BE
THE
LIGHT

A Blueprint for a Happy and Successful Life

Bill Halamandaris

LONGSTREET
Atlanta, Georgia

BE
THE
LIGHT

Published by
LONGSTREET, INC.
A subsidiary of Cox Newspapers
A subsidiary of Cox Enterprises, Inc.
2140 Newmarket Parkway
Suite 122
Marietta, GA 30067
www.lspress.com

Printed in the United States of America

1st printing 1999

Library of Congress Catalog Card Number: 99-61761

ISBN: 1-56352-565-8

Book and jacket design by Megan Wilson

For my teachers, the architects of this blueprint for life.
Thank you for your love and light.

Table of Contents

**BE
THE
LIGHT**

BE
THE
LIGHT

INTRODUCTION

"The search after the great man," Emerson wrote, "is the dream of youth and the most serious occupation of manhood." True to Emerson's words, my search for greatness began at an early age when as a boy I was encouraged to read the biographies of great men and women. There I began to consider the measure of greatness, the meaning and purpose of life.

This incipient interest grew into a passion that has dictated the direction of my life. It led me from a small mining town in Utah to the capital of our country, from an initial interest in law to a life of charity, from a career at the U.S. Senate to the establishment of the Caring Institute with my brother, Val, and, finally, beyond that to the creation of The Heart of America Foundation.

These two organizations were founded with many noble objectives and one highly personal purpose – to find, be near, and learn from the most successful human beings on the planet. With that determination, a magnificent odyssey began.

My quest has involved more than a quarter of a million nominators and hundreds of volunteer reviewers who helped evaluate the thousands of nominations received. Finally, the best of the best were scheduled for site visits and personal interviews.

We asked these people to tell us about their lives, what they do and why. We have asked them to describe the greatest lessons they have learned and tell us what life had taught them. We asked them what advice they would give others.

The lessons that follow are a product of this process. Each chapter reflects the learning and life experience of one or more of the most successful people in our country and a few remarkable souls from beyond our borders. It is a prescription for a happy and successful life and a blueprint for living.

This is the road map I sought as a boy. It has been drawn like a mosaic from the lives and understanding of people who are successful in the fullest sense of the word. For, "After all," as one of them, Truett Cathy, founder and president of Chick-fil-A, reminds us, "the goal is not to be successful in one aspect of our lives. The goal is to be successful in every aspect of our lives."

Each of our teachers offers a specific lesson, but it is what they have to say collectively that is most important. Collectively, they demonstrate the depth of human possibilities. If Ranya Kelly, a housewife working out of her home, can generate millions of dollars of support for those in need every year; if Tommie Lee Williams, a blind black man from Mississippi, can find a way to support his community for more than a quarter of a century; if one woman, Lois Lee, can save eight thousand children from the streets; if one man, Bob Macauley, can generate more than $2 billion worth of aid for people in need around the world – nothing is impossible.

These people show us how much one man or woman can do and remind us we could do more. They challenge us to follow and show us the way. They remind us, in the words of B. C. Forbes, that, "there can be no real success apart from service."

They also show us the well of goodness at the heart of America. For fifteen years, I have been blessed to be able to drink daily from this well. It is a greater gift than I can express. It gives me peace. It gives me hope. It gives me, as one of my friends likes to say, an antidote to the evening news. When others turn off the TV in disgust or watch with growing despair, I find comfort in the fact that I can identify someone – some individual – who is doing something substantial and significant about any problem you can name.

As you read what follows, I encourage you to put that conclusion to a test. Think of the problems we face and consider the power of one. Homelessness is a major problem in every city of size in our society, but look at what Father Joe, John, and Bea have done. So many in this country and around the world go to bed hungry, but Bob, Larry, Ferdinand and Stan have each found a way to feed millions. When our children are lost, abandoned, and abused, see what Lois, Dave, Donnalee, and the Magees have done to make a difference in their lives. If you doubt you can do what they have done, if you doubt you can make a difference, consider Benjamin, the boy without a brain, and think again.

Contrary to popular opinion, the secret of success in life has more to do with our hearts than our heads. What makes us different is not our ability to think but our ability to love. It is the heart that is made in the image of God.

At our best, people, like candles, dispel the darkness. Be the light.

I KNOW YOURSELF

"OUR DEEPEST FEAR IS NOT THAT WE ARE INADEQUATE. OUR DEEPEST FEAR IS THAT WE ARE POWERFUL BEYOND MEASURE. IT IS OUR LIGHT, NOT OUR DARKNESS, THAT FRIGHTENS US. WE ASK OURSELVES, 'WHO AM I TO BE BRILLIANT, GORGEOUS, TALENTED AND FABULOUS?' ACTUALLY, WHO ARE YOU NOT TO BE?

"YOU ARE A CHILD OF GOD. YOUR PLAYING SMALL DOESN'T SERVE THE WORLD. THERE'S NOTHING ENLIGHTENED ABOUT SHRINKING SO THAT OTHER PEOPLE WON'T FEEL INSECURE AROUND YOU. WE WERE BORN TO MANIFEST THE GLORY OF GOD WITHIN US. IT'S NOT JUST IN SOME OF US; IT IS IN EVERYONE. AND AS WE LET OUR OWN LIGHT SHINE, WE UNCONSCIOUSLY GIVE OTHER PEOPLE PERMISSION TO DO THE SAME. AS WE ARE LIBERATED FROM OUR OWN FEAR, OUR PRESENCE AUTOMATICALLY LIBERATES OTHERS."

...NELSON MANDELA

Recognizing
Your Gifts

All of life and everything in life is a gift. Talent can be refined. Tendencies can be reinforced. But both talent and ability are given.

While the gift of life is general, it is also specific. Each of us is *uniquely* gifted.

For Mary Anne Kelly, the gift is in her pain and the grace that brings, while Wally Amos and Fred Matser have been given the gift of joyfulness. Mel Blount and Kevin Johnson have the gift of celebrity. The Simpsons and Tommie Lee Williams are grounded and sustained by their humility.

Evelyn duPont, Father Joe Carroll, and many others have more specific gifts. Evelyn duPont, an Olympic swimmer, found she learned how to swim so that she could teach others how to walk. Father Joe Carroll hustled the world until the hound of God caught up with him and forced his efforts beyond himself. Father Joe said he always knew he would make millions, but he never dreamed it would be for the poor.

Everyone is needed. Everyone can contribute. God has given each of us the capacity to achieve some end necessary to others. No one is without the possibility of giving of himself as a human being.

In that fundamental fact can be found much of the joy of life. As Henry Emerson Fosdick wrote, "The Sea of Galilee and the Dead Sea come from the same source. It flows down clear and cool from the Heights of Hermon and the roots of the Cedars of Lebanon. The Sea of Galilee makes of it great beauty, while the Dead Sea creates only horror. The difference is the Sea of Galilee has an outlet. It gets to give."

The Gift of Life

"What we do for ourselves dies with us – what we do for others remains and is immortal."

...Albert Pike

On his eightieth birthday, Kurt Weishaupt threw himself a party. It was a lavish affair at the Waldorf Astoria for a thousand of his closest friends.

For Kurt the party was designed as an expression of his gratitude. Rather than bring him gifts, Kurt asked his guests to make a contribution to one of his *sixty* favorite charities. Including the matching amount Kurt personally contributed, that evening generated more than $1 million to support worthy causes ranging from the Salvation Army to the Gift of Life.

"I'm getting more satisfaction out of giving it than they will ever get out of receiving it," Kurt said the following morning. "If you accumulate a lot of money just to have a lot of money, that's waste paper. It doesn't serve any purpose."

Kurt's purpose is to give back some part of what he has received. "When I was in great danger," he explains, "there were lots of people who risked their own life to save us. We came to the conclusion that we owe something to those people and to this country which gave us a chance when the world was shut down and closed to us."

First in his memory is a priest in Marseilles who hid Kurt and his wife from the Gestapo and shepherded him to the Pyrenees where he escaped to Spain. But the most significant event in his life occurred in Spain as Kurt and his wife took a train to Madrid.

All they had was a ticket. Their money – British pounds – had been declared invalid by the British because of German counterfeiting. Kurt and his wife traveled at risk, with forged documents, and literally without a penny to their name.

"At that time, I had a Czech passport which I had picked up in Marseilles," Kurt said. "When the conductor and a Gestapo officer came through the train they looked at my passport and the Gestapo man immediately recognized it was a forgery."

Kurt still trembles when he recalls the terror of hearing the man from the Gestapo call out: "This is a false document!" He knew they were caught.

At that moment the door to a nearby first-class compartment opened. Before Kurt could respond to the Gestapo, he heard a man say, "Don't molest these people. They are my friends."

As if by magic, the conductor saluted and the Gestapo withdrew. Their benefactor stood up and called them into his compartment. He asked them to sit down and told them everything would be all right.

"He took us to Madrid," Kurt said. "He brought us to a hotel. He paid the bill in advance. He even bought some grapes for my wife. The next day, he picked us up in the afternoon, showed us Madrid, and then took us to dinner."

The following morning the Good Samaritan returned. He escorted the Weishaupts to the train station. He arranged travel, purchased tickets, gave them some documents and three thousand pesetas for the journey.

"When we came to the Portuguese border," Kurt said, "we were again asked to present our passports. Everyone else on the train had to get out. But we were allowed to continue."

"I never knew who that man was," Kurt said. "For fifty-two years, I have been asking myself, what moved this man who didn't know us to open the door and say – 'Don't molest those people'? It was like a higher power had transported him there for that particular moment. There is no other explanation."

In the half-century since, Kurt has sought many times to find his benefactor and thank him. A casual request from a friend for assistance in selling a stamp collection led to a lucrative career as a dealer and a personal fortune of some size, but the more Kurt prospered, the more obligated he felt to find a way to repay his unknown friend for the life he had been given.

What would the Spaniard say if he knew how his acts of kindness had been multiplied? How would he respond to Kurt's thanks and the knowledge that the man whose life he had saved had saved so many others, bringing hundreds of critically ill children from around the world to the United States for surgery? What would he say if he knew that the man he had fed and clothed fifty years ago had since found, fed, and clothed thousands in equal need?

I suspect he would respond much as Kurt responds to those who applaud his humanitarianism. "What I did, I did for myself," he says. "I don't expect any thanks for it. And I don't care what they say about me thirty years from now. What do I care about that? It is what happens now that counts."

QUESTIONS:

The highest purpose of humanity is to justify the gift of life. Kurt Weishaupt is acutely aware of his obligation to an unknown bene-factor. If you think about it, all of us have been given that same gift. Our stories may be less dramatic than Kurt's, but they are no less miraculous. Like Kurt, we have a duty to repay this fundamental debt. What progress have you made? Who helped make you who you are? How have you repaid them?

THE GIFT OF WHO YOU ARE

"Do what you can, with what you have, where you are."

...Theodore Roosevelt

If you ask Rita Ungaro Schiavone to describe herself, she will start simply. "I am a good wife and mother," she will tell you. "I'm a good child to my parents. I dote on my grandchildren."

Many would take her at her word and dismiss her with the conclusion that she is "just an average housewife."

Perhaps she would have been nothing more – valuable, but not remarkable – if twenty-two years ago, this good woman had not followed her concern, wondered about a neighbor, and walked into a dark house where that neighbor lived alone. What she saw changed her life.

"What I saw was an elderly woman, slightly built, sitting on the side of the bed," Rita said. "Her legs were dangling and you could tell they were atrophied from disuse. She explained to me she was blind and couldn't get up."

Rita chatted with her for a while and learned the woman had crippling arthritis and had lost her vision. She was nearly catatonic with depression.

The room was hot and stuffy. When Rita went into the kitchen to get the woman something cold to drink, she noted there was some dog food, but no dog in sight. There was no milk, soda, juice, or bread in the refrigerator.

That evening, Rita found her neighbor was still on her mind as she prepared the family dinner. She decided to make an extra portion for her new friend.

"I was preparing a nice, nourishing meal for my family," Rita remembers, "I thought I would share what we were having with her, rather than give her some canned goods she probably would never use."

From that simple, human instinct has come a network of women in Philadelphia who do what good women have always done. Each of them – some forty-five hundred strong – cook an extra portion for unseen friends when they prepare their family dinner. Aid for Friends, Rita's program, picks up the meals and arranges for storage and distribution through an extensive network of churches in a five-county area.

The first food center was set up in Rita's house. Now there are more than three dozen. The first Aid for Friends storage center was her freezer. Now there are more than seventy freezers and a walk-in box supporting the effort. Rita, once petrified to speak at her son's PTA, has now spoken to more than a quarter of a million people and recruited volunteers from seventy Catholic churches, seventy Protestant churches and a dozen synagogues.

Rita's message is simple: "Everyone can do something. If you don't want to cook, you share your financial resources. You share your time. You drive and deliver, or you share a part of yourself as a visitor. If you cook, you just put a little aside. That's not much extra, not much effort. But just one meal adds up fast."

The last count I have says there are now over seventeen thousand volunteers in Rita's network of friends. Their individual efforts add up to more than eight hundred thousand meals a year for poor, isolated, and homebound elderly clients.

When I asked her what she has learned from all this, Rita said, "People have to realize they have power. God gave them power. We have the power to do things and change things. We can change people's lives."

"Through it all," Rita says, "I sort of found out that this was what I was supposed to do with my life. I wasn't supposed to use all my spare time just swimming or ice skating or just enjoying myself. And my life has meaning beyond my wildest imagination."

QUESTION:

It's hard to see yourself clearly. Spend some time looking for your unique gifts. What are your best qualities and attributes? Consider all aspects of your life – physical and spiritual, mental and emotional, personal and professional.

The Gift of What You Do

"Always take your heart to work."

...Meryl Streep

"All the passions that people talk about, sometimes glibly, like love, compassion, and concern, all of those kinds of things are embodied in the face of a child," Bill Magee says. "And when you see a child that's hopeless and you know that you have the capability, whether it's the financial capability or an educational capability or a technical capability to change the life of that child, when you feel that and mist comes into your eyes, or tears come down your cheeks, that's when you are stirred into action. That's when that passion that exists in your heart takes on a fire of its own."

Magee's passion has to do with changing the world – one face at a time. The son of a physician, Bill Magee went to dental school because his advisors told him he wasn't smart enough to go to medical school. After graduating from dental school with honors, he went on to medical school largely to prove his counselors wrong. Then in 1981, Bill, now a gifted plastic surgeon, and his wife, Kathy, a nurse and social worker, were invited to participate in what was to be a life-changing event – a medical mission to the Philippines.

"We were somewhat naive," Kathy remembers. "We just kind of packed our bags and met everyone in L.A. and off we went to the Philippines."

What they found shocked them to the core.

"We had just never seen so many children with so many

needs. We were able to help about forty children. But when we left, there were still two hundred standing in line waiting for us."

The hospital administrator told them as they left, "If you can come back someday, the children will still be here. They may be five years older, but they will still be waiting."

By the time they had arrived home, the Magees had already decided they were going to go back to Naga City. The faces of the children haunted them and they knew they had to do something, but they had no idea how.

"We just said, 'Gee, there are a lot of kids there who need help,'" Kathy remembers. "So, we decided we'd go back and take care of those kids. We knew we would need supplies, but we figured we could get a few supplies."

Since then the images of broken faces, hearts, and lives have fueled over 120 medical missions to fifteen countries. The Magees and their associates have performed over twenty thousand surgeries abroad and an equal number here in the United States. There are now twenty-five Operation Smile chapters in the United States. Missions depart from the United States monthly to distant villages in Kenya, Ecuador, China, Vietnam, Nicaragua, Panama, the Philippines, Russia, the Middle East, Colombia, Venezuela, and Romania.

Reflecting on what Operation Smile has become, Bill says, "I think most of us never recognize the most significant moments of our lives when they are happening. It's obvious that our first visit to the Philippines – that drastic moment with the image of 250 families coming at you, every kid in the family tugging at your sleeve and every parent begging you to take care of their child, compounded by the knowledge that if we didn't take care of them, they were going to live a life of shame – had a profound impact. But when I look back, it's equally obvious that there were so many steps that led up to the Philippines, so many things, so many little decisions that led us there."

What really happened in the Philippines, he says, is that they came to a conclusion there was a pattern to their lives, they came to the realization that all the knowledge they had received and all the opportunities that they had been given had been given for a purpose.

"That's the power of Operation Smile," Bill concludes. "It transcends that child, and it really speaks to the best of the spirit that's in each of us. In a child's face you see torture and despair and hopelessness. Forty-five minutes later there is beauty and joy and a future.

"Each of us only has a small bit of the puzzle. But each of us has at least one piece."

QUESTIONS:

If the talents you have, the gifts you can identify, have only been directed at yourself and serve no purpose beyond your own needs, your true gift has not been actualized. Bill Magee discovered the reason he was forced to get to medical school through dental school when he realized both skills were needed in the fields of the Philippines. What is the best use, the highest purpose of each of your gifts? How could they best be applied in combination?

THE POWER OF ONE

"For each of us, there is only one thing necessary, to
fulfill our own destiny according to God's will to be
what God wants us to be."

                                        ...*Thomas Merton*

The Power of Positive Thinking has sold over seven million
copies and been translated into fifteen languages since it was
first published in 1952. "Forty some years ago when I wrote
The Power of Positive Thinking," Dr. Norman Vincent Peale
said with a smile, "I was widely criticized by scientists. Now
those same scientists have adopted it and given it a long
technical name."

The message of *The Power of Positive Thinking* has become
so much a part of our culture that we take it for granted. Yet,
for many, Dr. Peale's theories reflect the greatest revolution of
our generation – the discovery that human beings, by changing the inner attitudes of their minds, can change the outer
aspects of their lives.

Charles Swindoll wrote, "Attitude is that 'single string' that
keeps me going or cripples my progress. It alone fuels my fire
or assaults my hope. When my attitude is right, there is no
barrier too high, no valley too deep, no dream too extreme, no
challenge too great for me."

Dr. Charles Garfield's studies of peak performers identified
a positive mental attitude as the single most common characteristic of men of achievement.

When I met Dr. Garfield I couldn't resist asking him who

had impressed him the most of all the businessmen, politicians, sports figures, and artists he had studied. His answer was illuminating.

Garfield didn't give me the name of any of the powerful executives or political leaders he had interviewed. He said instead that the person who had impressed him the most was Dr. J. – Julius Erving – the hall-of-fame basketball player. When I asked him why, Garfield responded without hesitation, "Because when I asked him how high he could jump, his response was, 'How high do I have to?'"

Such was the power of Dr. J's attitude that he clearly believed he could do anything he wanted to – and did, much as Michael Jordan now does. He embodied Dr. Peale's fundamental belief – "What you believe, you achieve."

What Dr. Peale teaches us is that we all tend to grow to resemble our expectations of ourselves. More often than not, he reminds us, these expectations for ourselves are shaped by other's expectations of us. We all have the power to positively influence each other's lives and to bring out the best in each other.

You can test Dr. Peale's conclusion by examining your own life. What did you hear from the top of the stairs? When your parents, sisters and brothers, and friends talked about you, what did they say? How did their perception of you influence you and shape what you believe and became?

Since we always have a choice, Dr. Peale suggests we accentuate the positive. "I have found that if one looks for the best in every person, the best will reveal itself," he said. "People mold us. They can inspire us, depress us, or excite us. So build up as many people as you can. Do it unselfishly. Do it because you like them and because you see possibilities in them. Never miss an opportunity to say a word of congratulations upon anyone's achievement, or express sympathy in sorrow or disappointment."

Every test, every study and scientific examination tells us every human being has more potential than he or she has ever demonstrated. This distance, the difference between where we are and what we can be, is our challenge.

QUESTIONS:

How great is the distance from where you are to what you are capable of being? What can you do to close that gap?

YOU CAN'T BEAT GOD AT GIVING

"The magnanimous know very well that they who give time, or money, or shelter to a stranger put God under obligation to them – so perfect are the compensations of the universe."

...Emerson

When I first heard about Sweet Alice Harris, I thought that her name was rather unusual. After I met her, it was clear there is nothing else you could call her. She has the kind of smile that breaks through and warms you to your toes.

I found her in the heart of Los Angeles where she runs a program called the Parents of Watts. The literature said Parents of Watts provides emergency shelter and meals for homeless men and women, run a custodial care facility for unwed mothers, and teach parenting skills to teenage mothers.

That didn't seem possible based on the resources identified. There were no big corporate donors or government grants going to the project. I decided to get there early to look around before my interview with Sweet Alice.

I arrived around seven o'clock on a cool spring morning and was surprised to find a girl sleeping on Sweet Alice's porch. The girl was about fifteen and at least six months pregnant.

When I asked, I learned she had arrived in the middle of the night after a fight with her mother. She said she had chosen to sleep outside rather than ring the bell and wake Sweet Alice. I later learned this was not an isolated occurrence – such is the respect Sweet Alice commands in her community.

Over a quarter of a century, Sweet Alice put together a complex of ten buildings dedicated to meeting all of the essential needs of her urban neighbors – from literacy to food and shelter. But her favorite accomplishment is an eighteen-student high school housed in one of the homes in the complex. Sweet Alice routinely sends more kids on to college from this small facility than does the Watts public high school down the street.

"When I hear people say, 'Well, I'm on my feet and I did mine myself,' I get upset," Sweet Alice said. "You didn't do nothing by yourself. You didn't bring yourself into the world. Nobody gets where they are by themselves. Somebody had to help them."

In Sweet Alice's case, that somebody was the woman who took her in, told her she had worth, employed her, and helped raise her as a teenager. "They got me from the street," Sweet Alice recalls. "Ms. Anne said to me, 'There's a million-dollar smile on your face and that means there is something in you. I want to help you. What do you want to be?' I wouldn't be here except for her."

"That's what life is about," Sweet Alice said. "Somebody had to clean up your vessel. Somebody helped you. Somewhere down the line, we have forgotten that. When I'm gone, I want you all to say she fed somebody. She clothed somebody. I was somebody's friend."

When Sweet Alice first thought about helping others, she had nine children and one source of extra income – a second house that she rented out. "I said I would start a program and I would help people because I understand what they are going through. I understand how they feel. I know how to help them because God had me wear the shoes first. I wanted to help them, but I didn't know how. I didn't have any resources. I didn't have anything to give up. Then something said to me, 'You've got a house over there you rent out. Start a program there.'"

For Sweet Alice, this was the test of her commitment. She looked at the needs of her community and said, "Lord, I guess I better give up this house because we really need a program. Our young people are killing one another and our old people are back in the house hiding like they don't see what's going on. We need to do something and it has to start with me. I cannot expect anybody else to do anything while I am sitting back here and holding mine for a rainy day. Let me give up mine and when I give mine, then I can come to you and say, I gave all I had.

"When I gave up that house, guess what happened? God has blessed us with nine more houses. We are just a vessel that God uses to do his work," she concludes. "He fills up the vessel and we are then to give of it where it is needed. If your vessel gets filled up and you don't give it out, then God can't put nothing else in. If you give out, he will beat you. You can't beat God at giving."

QUESTIONS:

Are you holding something back? What are you afraid to risk? How could these resources best be employed and what difference would it make?

Understanding How You Make a Difference

All of us want to make a difference. We would like to think that there is a purpose to our lives and that the world will somehow benefit from our birth — though we may not know how.

When we think of how we might make a difference, however, we tend to think in terms of cataclysmic events and heroic acts. It is easier to see the impact of a single act of heroism than to assess the impact of a lifetime of kindness.

But more often than not, we make a difference not by some heroic act of momentous consequence but by small, sustained acts of caring and compassion. There is as much value in a lifetime of caring for people with cancer as there is in finding a cure for cancer.

If you doubt that fact, consider the example of Mother Teresa. Has anyone in this generation made a greater contribution to society? Is there any solitary act, however brave, however noble, that can compare?

Caring is an act of will as well as an act of love. The most fundamental law of human nature is that we cannot love without giving and it is in loving and giving that we find meaning and purpose for our lives.

Everyone Makes a Difference

"Be faithful to that which exists nowhere but in yourself."

...Andre Gide

Rachel Rossow has twenty-one children and lives in Connecticut. Though she would not acknowledge any distinction – to her, a child of choice, emerging from the heart, is as much hers as a child of the body – society would say that nineteen of her twenty-one children are adopted. Most of them are severely handicapped, including Benjamin, who was born without a brain.

When Benjamin was born, the learned men of medicine at the hospital decided there was no point to his life. A child without a brain cannot contribute, cannot function, cannot sustain himself. With nothing more than a brain stem to guide his actions, he would never be a doctor or a lawyer. His potential quality of life was judged so limited it was said he could hardly function – let alone make a difference.

No one asked Benjamin, of course, and if they had, he could not have responded. But Rachel answered for him, reaching out and taking him home to be part of her remarkable family. Eleven years ago when I came to know Benjamin, he had become one of the most powerful teachers I have ever met.

When Rachel introduced me to her son, I saw him respond in ways the medical establishment said would not be possible when he was born, and still cannot explain. He tracked her with his eyes, responded to her embrace, and laughed when she laughed. He not only knew *who* she was, he knew *where* she was all the time.

He will never run with a football or even walk by himself, but Benjamin has become an overachiever. He is performing at 150 percent of capacity. He is a pure person who knows nothing of prejudice, has never learned to hate, and will never even dream of harming another person. He knows only love and that love – the love he has been given and the love he gives – has enabled this child, who, it was said, would never make a difference, to change the Baby Doe laws in two states.

QUESTIONS:

*Benjamin's lesson is that everyone matters. Everyone makes a difference. The only question is one of degree and direction. What you can do, only you can do. What you can do, you **must** do now or it will remain undone. Who has benefited from your birth? What is your contribution to the world?*

EVERYONE CAN BE GREAT

"Goodness is not tied to greatness, but greatness to goodness."

...Thomas Moffett

By the time he was twenty-nine years old, Millard Fuller was a millionaire. Along with a friend from law school, he had developed a direct mail and publishing business into an enterprise that made its owners hundreds of thousands of dollars a year.

"I lived in a lovely home, drove a Lincoln Continental, had a cabin cruiser and speedboats on a nearby lake, and owned about two thousand acres of prime pasture land with riding horses and herds of cattle. I pursued a life of material things and justified it in my own mind by saying that later on in my life I would start caring again," Millard recalls.

Just when he thought he had it all, he lost everything that mattered. Millard came home to find a note from his wife. She told him she was taking the kids and leaving him.

"I gave her everything that money could buy, but me," he explains, "and she left me. I married a girl I was very much in love with and then promptly abandoned her for a life of material things."

Realizing his mistake, Fuller followed her and out of their reconciliation came a decision to start a new life. "I learned that possessions do not bring happiness, nor do they give meaning to life," he says.

Millard sold his business. He gave the money away and began looking for a better way to live.

On the way back from visiting family in Florida, the Fullers stopped to visit a friend at the Koinonia Farm near Americus, Georgia. They had planned to stay a couple of hours, but wound up staying a month, captivated by Clarence Jordan, one of the founders of the Farm and a charismatic Christian leader.

In August 1968, Fuller and Jordan called fifteen people together for a meeting to talk about local housing problems. Out of their discussion came a concept based on the biblical adage of building houses for the poor while "seeking no profit and charging no interest." The concept was later called Habitat for Humanity.

"We don't have shacks and substandard housing because there's not money enough," Fuller says now. "We have shacks because there are not enough people who care enough to make it an unacceptable solution."

With the help of volunteers and seed money from donations, the partners began building the first tract of twenty-seven houses in Americus, Georgia. For a minimal down payment and a commitment of "sweat equity" – participation in the building process – low-income families were promised a decent house and an interest-free mortgage. The mortgage payments, often lower than the rent families had been paying for the shacks they lived in, were used to fund the construction of more houses.

The original tract was completed in 1972. Today, Habitat has become one of the largest home builders in the world. Its goal is the total elimination of poverty housing.

When I asked Millard if he ever regretted leaving the law and the world of business, he responded, "The greatest pay-offs are not in money. Materialism is like cotton candy at a carnival. It looks good. But when you bite into it, there is nothing there. The things that mean the most to most people are not monetary things. Ultimate values are not tied up with material possessions. I don't care how much money you've got, when you die the only thing that you leave behind is what you have given away.

"I think Martin Luther King had it right," Millard concludes. "Everybody can be great, because everyone can serve.

That's the measure of greatness. Nobody has any chance of being thought really great a century from now except those who have been the servants of us all."

QUESTIONS:

Millard Fuller gave up his millions to be with his wife and pursue a higher calling. Those were his priorities. What are yours? Is there something or someone you would you give up all your material possessions for? Who or what means the most to you?

The hands are the best examination of the conscience. In the words of Marcus Aurelius, "Every man is worth just as much as the things he busies himself with." What did you do today? What do you busy yourself with? What do you spend most of your time doing? Think tasks, not titles.

LEARN TO LOVE

"The love of our neighbor is the only door out of the dungeon of self."

...George Macdonald

Ranya Kelly is a middle-class housewife living in a suburb of Denver. As she recalls it, she learned the lesson of love just before Christmas about twelve years ago.

"I was looking for a box to do some Christmas shipping and I came across five hundred pairs of shoes in a dumpster behind a mall," she says. "I couldn't believe what I saw."

Later that evening, Ranya came back with her husband and picked all the shoes out of the trash, took them home, and spread them out on the floor. After giving as many shoes away to her friends and family as possible, Ranya found she still had hundreds more. She decided to take the rest down to a local shelter.

"I never knew about the shelters or people in need," Ranya said. "I grew up in an upper-middle-class family. I was never involved with people. I was just thinking of somewhere I could drop these shoes off so they wouldn't go to waste."

But what she saw at the shelter changed her life. "There was a woman standing in the doorway," Ranya says, "her pants dragging on the floor. She had a little baby, about two or three, with her. She was pregnant and barefoot in the middle of January. I couldn't believe it. The look in her eye and her gratitude changed my life."

The Shoe Lady, as Ranya is now known, manages to find and distribute more than $2 million worth of shoes and other merchandise to people in need each year. She does this out of her suburban home, operating on a budget of less than twelve thousand dollars a year.

She serves as a liaison between those who need help and area businesspeople who can provide it. She has secured deals with dozens of companies including JC Penney, Med-i-Save, and Builders Square.

"We all have this need to be needed," Ranya says. "If we are not responsible for something, we are kind of lost. The more I got involved with people, the more I felt needed and the happier I became."

QUESTION:

Follow your love. What small step can you take that might improve the life of someone near you?

THE JOY OF SERVICE

"Human beings are not fully happy or healthy until they serve the purpose for which God created them."

...Ken Carey

When I wrote to tell JoAnn Cayce she had been nominated for national recognition, JoAnn responded: "I don't know this fellow that's nominated me (he happened to be the mayor of an adjacent town) and I don't know what I've done that he thinks is so special. I'm just doing what my mother and grandmother have done before me. And besides, I don't have much use for awards anyway. The president wanted to give me an award last year and I told him to put it in the mail."

For six months after her letter, JoAnn wouldn't talk with me. She was too busy taking care of the poor to be bothered talking about it.

Finally, one hot summer day we got together at her home in a wide spot in the road, called Thornton, Arkansas. When I asked her why she did what she did, she told me her earliest memories are of her mother taking care of people.

"My mother always saw after everybody who couldn't see after themselves. We never knew who would be eating or sleeping with us. She would take in prostitutes, alcoholics, anyone. She was always filling out papers for them, taking people food or clothing, whatever. In her later years she would get up in the morning and put on a big pot of turnip greens or beans or soup and she would watch the people coming down this road out here to see who might be hungry."

JoAnn has been the conscience of her community for more than forty years. A one-woman Salvation Army, she does what needs to be done, sometimes for up to twenty hours a day, for the poor in the four counties surrounding the little town of Thornton, Arkansas. It is a mark of her impact that many government agencies refer problems they can't solve to her.

"I do nothing," she said as she surveyed the contents of one of her two storage sheds. "All this stuff has been given to us. I'm just a tunnel it flows through. It didn't come from me. It comes from caring people. A lot of them, I never see. I don't even know how they find out about me, but they will come here and bring things or drop them off on the porch."

She points toward the dresser and says, "I have in that bowl over there an envelope with $3.57 that a woman from Pine Bluff – and that is fifty-four miles from here – dropped off. She left me a note that said she was on her way to a family reunion and wanted me to take this money and buy some child school supplies with it.

"Everybody has got a purpose," JoAnn says. "Look at the poor. They make me feel needed. They have done for me more than I will ever do for them. They have given me purpose.

"What would I do with my life if I didn't have people who needed me? Play bridge? Collect dolls and clean house? Anybody can dust!

"I think people need to know it's just a joy to be alive and to be of service to somebody. I don't care what you are doing. If there is not happiness and satisfaction in it and you have to be mad at the world, you are in the wrong business. You ought to do something else, like I do. I have told my children, I never want them to say, 'Mother worked herself to death for the poor.' I am doing exactly what I want to do. Mrs. Rockefeller hasn't had near what I have had.

"I don't care how poor you are, you can help somebody," JoAnn concludes. "When you want to find a way, there is a way. You don't ever have to be afraid to do what is in your heart or be ashamed or embarrassed that you love somebody and want to help them."

QUESTIONS:

Joseph Campbell advises those looking for direction to "follow your bliss." What do you do for fun? What part of your day do you look forward to and most enjoy? How can you do more of that?

THE GOLDEN YEARS

"When you cease to make a contribution, you begin to die."

...Eleanor Roosevelt

In 1965, they sent Sister Mary Luca to Phoenix to retire. She had worked as a teacher in parochial schools for forty-five years, and they thought that was enough. It was time for her to rest.

No one asked her if she was ready to retire, of course, probably because if they had she would have told them what she told me: "I think we should take that word out of the vocabulary," she said. "It's dumb. I don't want to hear it."

Sister Luca started looking for something useful to do. She found her calling when she visited the Mexican school in the barrio. "I never saw so much poverty," she recalled. Everywhere Sister Luca went, she saw hurting people in need. It didn't take her long to decide she wanted to do something about it.

It began simply. She would see a youngster who needed a shirt or a blouse and then ask one of the women of the parish to help her go out and find it.

By the time we met, the odd shoe and shirt she had fallen into collecting had grown to a clothing program. She was providing school clothes for over ten thousand children a year, finding food for those in need, providing help with emergency rent and utilities, medical care, and summer employment.

Twenty-two years after her "retirement," God's Lady in

Arizona, as she came to be known, was still at it. She had a hip replaced, bad feet, fragile bones, and arthritis like so many others at the senior center where she lived. But she refused to "rest."

"I'm like the Eveready bunny," she said. "I just keep going."

When her vision deteriorated to the point where she was a menace on the highway, the courts provided her with a driver and an assistant. Criminals were sentenced to work with her and escort her around.

When I asked her how much longer she planned to continue, she said, "As long as I can! If nothing else, I'll be working in the infirmary taking care of the older sisters." Sister Luca was eighty-three at the time. Her smile indicated she intended the irony in her remark.

At the time of Caesar the average life span was thirty-three years. A child born in 1900 could only anticipate living until the age of forty-three. It was in this context that Bismarck fixed the retirement age at sixty-five. Few people then alive were expected to live so long.

Thanks to the miracles of modern science, our life span nearly doubled over the last century. A child born today can expect to live until the age of seventy-eight, and many people will live far into their second century.

What will we do with this gift? As Sister Luca would say, "That's a long time to play golf.

"Think of other people," she urges. "Because we are not in this world just for ourselves. Don't think of yourself all the time. Get out and do something for other people. Because when you start thinking about yourself, you pity yourself, and then the next thing you know you've got aches and pains and what not, and you start crabbing. You've got to think of other people."

In the words of Watterson Lowe, "Nobody grows old by merely living a number of years. People grow old only by deserting their ideals. Years wrinkle the face, but to give up enthusiasm wrinkles the soul."

Richard Bach offered this test to find whether your mission on earth is finished. "If you are alive," he said, "it isn't." Your journey is not over, your task is not complete.

QUESTIONS:

We prepare all of our lives for the Golden Years, postponing enjoyment and investing resources. What is the best use of the investment you have made in yourself and your future? What have you learned that you can employ after you retire for the benefit of others? What skills, talents, and interests do you have that you can share?

Finding
Your Way

Mother Teresa was a teacher at a
church-sponsored school in India
before beginning her work with
the Missionaries of Charity. As
she contemplated this "career
change," she asked her counselor, "How will I know when I
have found my place?"

"You will know by your happiness," came the response.

You will know you are in the right place when everything you have done seems to have prepared you for what you are doing. You will know when you find yourself fully engaged. You will know when you have an avenue to employ your unique abilities and find yourself fulfilled. You will know by the joy and happiness it brings.

If that is how the journey ends, how does it begin?

H E A R   T H E   W H I S P E R

"I have no special revelation of God's will. He reveals himself daily to every human being, but we shut our ears to the 'still small voice.'"

...Gandhi

Rick Julian's early years were marked by poverty and abuse. While others might have become bitter, angry, and unproductive under similar circumstances, Rick developed remarkable character and maturity at an early age.

When I first met him two years ago, all he had to his name was a pair of boxer shorts. He had lived in shelters or with distant relatives most of his life. He worked two part-time jobs to get by while he was in school.

Somehow, he still managed to become a star athlete and the class president. He also managed to devote significant amounts of his time to helping others. All through high school, Rick worked with the homeless, counseled abused children, and supported the local children's hospital with fund-raising drives.

Rick is quick to give credit to others. "You don't know how many people have done something to help me," he said. "I wouldn't be where I am without the help of literally thousands of caring people."

Where he is at the moment is at college. He is there on scholarship, playing quarterback on the football team and holding down a perfect 4.0 average.

Though he still has nothing of material value whatsoever, he will tell you what he does have is more important. He has God-given talent, the desire to use that talent in a way that helps others, and God's guiding voice. In the many quiet moments when he was alone, Rick has learned that God speaks to us in the silence of the heart.

"But you have to learn to listen," he says.

Rick learned this lesson from a friend and counselor at one of the many shelters he has occupied. "We were in town one day," Rick said, "and suddenly he grabbed my arm. We stopped and my friend said, 'Listen.'

"There were sounds of the city all around me, but that seemed unremarkable, so I asked him, 'Why?'

"My friend said, 'I hear a cricket.'

"I thought he was crazy. There were cars honking, people rushing by, and trucks passing. I could hardly hear our conversation. But my friend insisted and walked toward a flower bed nearby. Sure enough, there under the branch of an azalea bush, he found a cricket chirping away.

"I was totally amazed. I told my friend I thought he must have fantastic hearing, but he responded. 'No, not at all. It's just a question of what you are tuned into. Watch."

His friend reached into his pocket and dropped some coins on the sidewalk. He heard them fall – as did everyone else nearby. Rick watched as people stopped in their tracks. Some put their hands in their pockets. Others looked around in confusion.

"We are all like that," Rick concluded. "Too often we ignore what is really important. We look for the fire and miss the candle. We listen for God's shout and miss the whisper.

We have to learn to look for the candle. We have to learn to hear the whisper."

QUESTION:
Check your priorities. Are you tuned into what's really important in your life?

GOD WILL GET YOU

"Every man has a mission from God to help his fellow beings."

...*James Gibbons*

Sara O'Meara and Yvonne Fedderson met on *The Ozzie and Harriet Show* when they were cast as the girlfriends of the two Nelson boys. In 1959, they were on their way home from a USO tour in Korea when they stopped in Japan, right after a typhoon had struck the island.

"We walked out of the hotel one night and into the devastation that had occurred and found eleven children huddled together to keep warm," Sara says. "We had never seen anything like it."

Without thinking beyond the immediate implications of their actions, Yvonne and Sara took the children back to their hotel, gave them a hot bath, fed them, and then went looking for help. They soon learned a few orphan children were not a large concern in the midst of such devastation.

With the grudging help of the U.S. Army, Sara and Yvonne found a Japanese woman who agreed to take care of these children. The woman's small home became an orphanage. They recruited U.S. servicemen to repair the house and arranged to provide the woman and the children with all the essentials they would need.

Though they didn't know it at the time and, in fact, the idea of starting an organization was the furthest thing from their minds, Sara and Yvonne had taken the first step in starting Childhelp USA. Today Childhelp USA has taken the lead in providing solutions for abused and neglected children in this country. They operate a national hotline and have established several residential treatment centers for the victims of child abuse and neglect throughout the country.

"We try to be flexible, because we want God to lead this organization, as he always has," Yvonne says. "So even though we make plans, we stay open in case God has something different planned. We will follow his path."

Sara agrees and then speaks of the happiness they have found. "The only time people can be happy is when they give to others," she says. "Nothing material can make you completely happy on its own. It might make you comfortable, but giving to others, doing for others – that's where happiness really comes from."

There is a place and purpose for each of us. While we all travel together, we are each unique and have our own path. If you look at where the road leads you, if you listen with your heart, God will get you.

QUESTION:

Listen with your heart. Where is God leading you?

EVERYONE HAS A PURPOSE

"Remember: God loves me. I'm not here just to fill a
place. He has chosen me for a purpose."

...*Mother Teresa*

A former professional tennis player, businessman, and broker,
Stan Curtis was in hot pursuit of the "good life" when, he says,
God caught up with him. He had a life-changing experience
in a restaurant.

"It was my time, no doubt," Stan says. "Divine direction
sent me right to that restaurant at that moment."

Stan was in a Louisville cafeteria line and about to ask for a
spoonful of green beans when a waiter came by and took the
container away. The waiter replaced it with a new container of
beans, but Stan remembers thinking, "Those green beans
looked pretty good to me. Why are they taking them away?
What are they going to do with them?"

When that question would not leave him, he asked for the
manager and found out that the beans had been removed for no
better reason than that studies had indicated customers were
more likely to order when presented with heaping containers of

food. Before he knew it, Stan found himself wondering if he could find a way to get those green beans to someone who was hungry rather than just let them be thrown away.

"And that was it," Stan says. "You know, I'm not a saint, but really I believe people shouldn't be hungry in America – they shouldn't be hungry anywhere, but particularly not here where there is food to be had."

From that moment and that instinct came Kentucky Harvest – and from that, Harvest USA. Harvest USA now raises about two hundred million pounds of food a year. "All we do," Stan says, "is find it where it is and take it to where it is needed. From those who have it and don't want it, to those who want it and don't have it. We keep it simple. There is no reason to create any complication in the middle."

Keeping it simple means operating without staff or any formal administrative structure. If you would like to test that commitment, send them a check. Harvest USA will send it back.

When you ask him why, Stan will tell you it is because giving money is too easy. "What we want is your involvement," he adds. "We need your energy. We need your brain power. If you want to help feed people, don't give me a check. Give me an hour of your time."

Stan, who calls himself a bleeding-heart conservative, says, "I honestly had no idea I would be doing this. Eight years ago, I didn't give a damn about hunger or homelessness. I didn't care about anything but making money, a car, assets, and a golf handicap. That's it.

"I was thirty-six when I started Harvest. Now I'm sorry that it took me so long. When I think about Harvest now and what it has done for me, I just can't believe how full my life has become. It's a gift. I didn't know this was going to happen to me and one day it just happened."

QUESTION:
Have you found your purpose, your place in the world, or do you have a sense there is something more you should be doing?

GIVING IN TO GOD

"The highest form of worship is service to humanity."

...*Saint Vincent de Paul*

"Don't even think of me as Mother Teresa," Father Joe Carroll said. "She saw the hungry and the homeless and they touched her heart so that she had to do something for them. I ran into the Bishop's office and he dumped it on me. 'Bottom line,' he said, 'you're in charge of the homeless.' I had a 104-degree fever for a week.

"Give me the rationale," Father Joe asked the Bishop. "You are replacing me in my parish with a social worker and I, who know nothing about social work, am being moved here. I don't understand that."

The Bishop responded, "You can hire social workers. I need a guy who can find the money. I asked twelve priests who was the biggest hustler in the diocese. They all named you."

Father Joe laughs at that. "I have always been a wheeler-dealer," he says. "I have done everything. I have worked in laundries and fixed washing machines. I worked for the post office and in grocery stores. I worked in a butcher shop at the age of eight. I was a street kid. I just did whatever. I always knew I'd make millions – I just didn't think it would all be going to the homeless."

I met Father Joe in his modest office at the heart of St. Vincent de Paul Village, the best facility for the homeless in the country. When he acquiesced to the Bishop's will a dozen years ago, he began with an orientation trip to other homeless shelters across the country. He came back with a determination to do it right.

"I was embarrassed when I saw what they did," he recalls. "I said this is what we send people to? We build better places for the animals in the zoo. I just don't think that's the way you treat people.

"People tend to say, 'Look, they've got a place to sleep. It's indoors. That's good enough.' For me, it has to be nice or we won't build it. Christ said, 'If they are hungry feed them. If they are homeless, shelter them.' He didn't say, 'Make sure they need a meal.' He didn't say, 'The poor are any less human.' He didn't put all the strings and criteria on it that we have. They may do things I don't like, but ultimately you have to love them. You have to think, like Mother Teresa, you're doing something beautiful for God."

Somewhat to Father Joe's surprise, it worked. "When I went out with this idea. I kinda thought I was Robert Preston. You know – 'There's a problem here in River City. The problem is homelessness and we are going to do something about it.' And I knew it would never happen. 'We are going to build a first-class shelter for the poor.' It would never happen. It was the scam of scams. And people made the stupid thing happen."

Out of this Father Joe has built what is called the Taj Mahal of homeless shelters – St. Vincent de Paul Village. The complex covers more than a square city block, has a budget of $16 million a year, and cost more than $20 million to build.

"I fought it, but I finally accepted this role and the responsibility, because somewhere along the line you come to the conclusion that this is what God wants for you," Father Joe concludes. "You come up with all the arguments along the way – I'm not good enough, I am a sinner – all the reasons it won't work, all the reasons he shouldn't want you. Then you read the Scriptures and you see where he says, 'I choose the weak things of the world to show my greatness,' and you grit your teeth and give in. I think ultimately, that's it. I just gave in to God."

QUESTIONS:

Sometimes we do not recognize our talents because they seem so natural to us. They are so much a part of who we are, we take them for granted. What comes most easily to you? Is there some part of your life where you have reached what Maslow called "unconscious competence" – the highest level of skill development, the level of mastery?

A SIGN FROM GOD

"Only a life lived for others is worthwhile."

...Albert Einstein

Viktor Frankl is the only man I know who voluntarily entered the concentration camps.

When a friend told me about Frankl's *Man's Search for Meaning* I could hardly wait to find a copy. Now in its hundredth American printing, this slender volume has been named by the Library of Congress as one of the ten most influential books in America. I devoured it in less than an hour and was so moved by its message I have since given hundreds of copies to friends.

Because of my admiration for the author and his message, I sought the first opportunity to meet Dr. Frankl. Finally, about fourteen years ago, I succeeded. He became a friend and mentor who had a profound influence on my life.

Once in a quiet moment, he told me how he found his path, how he came to be in the concentration camps, and the value of that "abyss experience."

"When the Nazis came to power," he said, "I was the head of the neurological department of a Jewish hospital in Vienna. Anti-Semitism was increasing daily, and my family and I could see what was coming. Like many people, we began preparing to get out. I applied for a visa to come to America where I could continue my work.

"At the eleventh hour, as the Nazis were closing in, the U.S. Consulate informed me a visa had been granted for me to emigrate to the United States. This was the moment I had anticipated for several years and I rushed down to the consulate with great excitement. My enthusiasm fled when I realized the visa was only valid for one. I was confronted by the fact that if I escaped to America, I would have to leave my parents behind."

In despair Viktor left the embassy and walked in a daze to a park nearby. Covering the yellow Star of David he was compelled to wear on his chest so the Nazis would leave him alone, he sat on the park bench in agony. What should he do?

"On one hand," he said, "was safety, the opportunity to work, and nurture my 'brain child' — logotherapy. On the other hand, there was the responsibility to take care of my parents by staying with them in Vienna and, rather than leaving them to their fate, share it with them."

Viktor could not find an answer. What would his parents do if he left? What could he do if he stayed? Would it make any difference to them or would all be lost?

"At best, if I stayed with my family, I would have the opportunity to be with them and protect them from being deported but who knew for how long before the Gestapo came for us all?" Viktor said. "If I stayed, my work and theories would perish with me."

Viktor sat there and meditated for more than an hour. Finally, he realized he could not resolve the matter and got up to go home. He remembers thinking somewhat sarcastically as he left that if there ever was a time that a man could use a sign from God, this would be it. The issue was beyond human resolution.

Almost immediately upon entering his apartment, Frankl

noticed a stone, a piece of marble on the radio. He called his father and asked him, "What is this and why is it here?

"'Oh, Viktor,' my father said with some excitement. 'I forgot to tell you. I picked it up this morning on the site where the largest synagogue in Vienna stood before the Nazis burned it down.'

"'And why did you bring it home?' I asked.

"'Because I noticed that it is part of the two tablets whereon the Ten Commandments are engraved – you remember, above the altar?' my father said. In fact, one could see, on the piece of marble, one single Hebrew letter engraved and gilded. 'Even more,' my father said, 'I can tell to which of the Ten Commandments this letter refers because it serves as the abbreviation for only one.'

"I looked at it and had my answer," Viktor said. "It was the commandment that says, 'Honor thy father and thy mother.' At that moment, my decision was clear. I gave up my visa and stayed in Austria. A few months later, the hospital was closed by the Gestapo. My whole family was arrested and taken to the concentration camps. My mother died in the gas chamber of Auschwitz. My brother died in a coal mine near Auschwitz. My father suffered first from starvation and finally succumbed to pneumonia."

The only satisfaction in this was that Viktor was able to visit his father in his barracks and be with him in his final hours. As a physician, he could not help but notice the terminal lung edema setting in. He saw his father in pain. He heard his struggle for breath and knew when it was time to use the single ampoule of morphine he had smuggled into camp.

Viktor waited and watched until the morphine worked.

When it brought relief he asked his father if there was anything more he could do for him. They talked for a moment more, then his father fell peacefully into the sleep Viktor knew would be followed by death.

As he left for his own barracks, Viktor knew he would never see his father again, but rather than sadness, he found himself experiencing happiness to a degree he had never known before.

There in the concentration camps, the most miserable of experiences, Viktor found his greatest joy. He had honored his father. He had been there for him and stayed with him to the last and as a result had been able to ease his father's pain.

At the same time, in ways he could not have anticipated, the decision to enter the concentration camp advanced his career and established the credibility of his work. For it was there that Frankl found the laboratory to test and prove his theories.

Freud believed that if you subject the mass of humanity to deprivation, human differences would be minimized and man would be reduced to fundamental desires, animal instincts, and a single-minded pursuit of survival at all cost.

"Freud was spared to get to know the concentration camps," Viktor observed. "But we who were there saw not the uniformity he predicted. People became ever more different when confronted by such a tragic situation. They unmasked their real selves — both the swine and the saint.

"In truth, I found it is the orientation toward a meaning to fulfill in the future – after liberation – that more than any other factor gave people the greatest chance to survive even this abyss experience. It is evidence of what I have come to call the self-transcendent quality of a human being – that is, a truly human being is never primarily or basically concerned with himself or herself, or anything within himself or herself; but rather is reaching out of themselves, into the world, toward a meaning to fulfill or another human being to love."

QUESTIONS:

Are you reaching out with love? To whom? How wide is your embrace?

KNOWING YOUR RESPONSIBILITY

Response is at the root of the word responsibility. It is the constant and key question of life. Ten percent of life has to do what happens to us. The other ninety percent is shaped by how we respond.

Life confronts us at every opportunity. Every moment of every day forces a decision. What will we do? How shall we respond?

We must choose with the knowledge that we change the world with everything we do or do not do. For as Molière observed, "It is not only what we do, but also what we do not do, for which we are accountable."

Every right implies a responsibility; every opportunity, an obligation; every possession, a duty. We are responsible *to* the world and *for* the world, and the rendering of useful service is our common calling. We must act with the knowledge that we influence each other whether we want to or not, wherever and whenever our lives touch.

T H E   C H O I C E

"I know of no more encouraging fact than the unques-
tionable ability of man to elevate his life by conscious
endeavor."

...Henry David Thoreau

When Melissa Poe was eight she saw something that scared
her. She was watching a futuristic episode of a television program called *Highway to Heaven.* It suggested what the world
would look like in the next century if mankind did not mend
its ways.

Melissa was so upset by this program she decided something had to be done. She knew that it was her future they
were talking about and she didn't want to live like that.

In her innocence Melissa did what a lot of kids would do.
She went looking for the biggest person she could find to ask
for help. Melissa thought the president would be a good place
to start.

Melissa wrote a letter to the president telling him what she
had seen and expressing her concerns. The White House sent
her a form letter encouraging her to "just say no."

It wasn't the president's fault. The same thing would have
happened under any administration. The White House gets
thousands of letters each day. Handwritten letters from eight-
year-old girls just aren't usually taken seriously.

When Melissa realized the president wasn't going to do
anything about her concerns, she could easily have become

discouraged. She could have walked away from a problem the world would say was too big for her. She could have gone out to play. Instead, Melissa decided that if the president wasn't going to do something, she would.

She went down to a local outdoor advertising company and asked a salesman how much a billboard cost. He humored her and gave her a number. "I don't want just any billboard," Melissa replied. "I want a good one – one people will see." The salesman humored her again and gave her a bigger number.

With her target in mind, Melissa set to work. She did chores, sold lemonade, collected and returned bottles, and saved her allowance. Three months later she was back with a bag of quarters and said, "I want that billboard."

At this point, the salesman had no choice but to take her seriously. He called the manager. The manager asked her why she wanted the billboard and what she planned to do with it. When she told him, you can guess what happened – he gave it to her.

Out of that came a national billboard campaign that Melissa organized to call attention to the needs of our environment. By the time I came to know her four years later, she was presiding over an international club of more than three hundred thousand kids concerned about the environment.

The following year, Melissa was the youngest person invited to address the Summit on the Environment in Rio de Janeiro. Standing next to her and listening as she spoke to the leaders of the world was the president of the United States.

QUESTION:

Charles Dickens said, "No one is useless in the world who lightens the burdens of another." What choices have you made in the last year that have lightened the burdens of others, including the burden of caring for our environment?

I'd Rather Be a Sermon

"It is from our lives and not from our words that our religion must be read."

...Thomas Jefferson

"As a minister," Larry Jones says, "you are always telling people to help other people. You hope your message helps and that by telling people what to do you can make a difference. Then, at thirty-eight, I realized there was another way."

Larry discovered the path less traveled when he took a group of pastors to Haiti. Their intent was to go down there and work in a church for a week, then turn around and come back home. It was a routine trip. Something he had done many times before.

But this trip proved to be totally different. One night as he was returning to his hotel, a little boy approached Larry and asked for a nickel. When he asked the child why he wanted the money, the boy said he hadn't had anything to eat all day and he wanted to buy a roll.

"I went into the hotel and I was overcome," Jones said,

"because I am from Oklahoma and I knew we had thirty-five million metric tons of wheat stored in grain elevators out there. Yet here, not an hour and a half away by air, there was a child who didn't have a piece of bread to eat."

Jones felt compelled to action. True to his profession, he decided he would preach a sermon on the subject the following Sunday. He would raise people's consciousnesses. He would persuade somebody to do something.

"I thought it was a pretty good sermon with a powerful message," he remembers, "but when I looked around after the service, I realized there was nobody in the room but me."

That's when Larry Jones realized that if anyone was going to do something about this problem, it would have to be him. Jones took his story to the community and asked for help. "I just told people what happened," he said. To his surprise, farmers called in and gave him literally tons of wheat.

Today, Feed the Children provides supplemental meals for over eighty thousand people a day and operates in sixty-seven countries. True to his purpose, he has inspired and involved thousands of people in the process. "It all started with one little boy," Jones says with wonder. "None of this was planned."

"I realize now," he says, "that there is a big difference between telling people to help someone and showing them. There are a lot of people like me in the world who want to reach out to their neighbor, but don't know how."

As James Russell Lowell observed, "Every man feels instinctively that all the beautiful sentiments in the world weigh less than a single lovely action." Every act is a teaching act. Ultimately, our lives are our message.

QUESTIONS:

Have you been content to pray for relief and wait for somebody to do something or are you doing what you can? Are you potentially the answer to someone's prayers?

THE FIRST RULE OF CARING

"Our grand business is not to see what lies dimly at a distance, but to do what lies clearly at hand."

...*Thomas Carlyle*

When Dave Soukup was a judge, he found his greatest challenges in juvenile court.

"When you are trying a civil case," he said, "there are some difficult decisions to be made, but even if you are talking about two or three million dollars, when you finish the case you can go home and not take the case home with you.

"But juvenile court is different. . . .

"You are being asked to decide, for example, whether or not to remove a little three-year-old girl from her home. The facts in front of you indicate she was brought in over the weekend to the emergency room. All you have is a statement from the doctor who examined her saying he doesn't believe the bruises on the child occurred as a result of a fall like her mother said.

"The mother is in court and she tells you that the child really did fall and that these bruises are normal and, anyway, her boyfriend is no longer in the home and is never coming back. And there you are on a Monday morning being asked to make a decision based on nothing more than this, as to whether to take this little girl out of her home or leave her in a potentially hazardous situation.

"How do you know: Is he really gone? Did he beat her up? Is the child in physical danger going home? Without knowing that, do you take her away from the only mother and the only home she's ever known? That could be equally traumatic.

"When you are faced with ten to twelve life-changing decisions like that a day," Soukup says, "you begin to lose sleep. There was no one in the court to tell me from the child's standpoint what was going on. Without an objective voice speaking for this little girl it really is an impossible decision."

When Dave found himself waking up too often at four o'clock in the morning, he decided to find a solution. He asked his bailiff to call a few people who were involved with agencies that served kids in the Seattle area. He invited them to come to juvenile court to talk about the possibility of recruiting and training volunteers to speak for abused and neglected kids in juvenile court. "I just said bring a brown-bag lunch and we'd talk it over," Dave says.

"I walked into a lunchroom at noon expecting to see four or five people and there were fifty people there. The people we had contacted talked to their friends and they talked to others and it just snowballed. That's what's happened to this idea ever since."

There are currently over three hundred thousand kids in foster homes around the country. The program Dave designed, Court Appointed Special Advocates, has already touched most of them and his goal is to reach the rest.

"It's pretty stunning," he says. "Out of my simple desire to be able to get to sleep a little quicker has come some tens of thousands of volunteers all across the country. But it really shouldn't be surprising. Most people, given an opportunity to do something to effectively help the helpless, will respond. It is human nature, thank God, to want to do what we can to make things better."

QUESTION:

No one has any right to find life uninteresting or unrewarding who sees within the sphere of his own activity a wrong he can help remedy. Every man is responsible for all the good within the scope of his abilities. What wrong is there that you can help remedy?

THE URGENCY OF NOW

"Yesterday is gone. Tomorrow has yet to come. We have only today. Let us begin."

> *...inscription at the front door of*
> *Mother Teresa's house in Calcutta*

All worthwhile people have good thoughts, good ideas, and good intentions, but too often our good instincts are neglected. Too few of our thoughts are translated into action.

Time is our most precious commodity. You cannot do a kindness too soon, for you never know how soon it will be too late. In the words of Samuel Johnson, "Let him that desires to see others happy make haste to give while his gift can be enjoyed and remember that every moment of delay takes away something from the value of his benefaction."

No one understands the preciousness of the moment better than Bob Macauley. Because of this he founded AmeriCares largely on the principle of instantaneous response to worldwide needs and disasters. Starting in one room with two staffers, AmeriCares has raised and distributed more than $2 billion worth of aid for those in need around the world. Often AmeriCares is in the air with desperately needed medicine, supplies, and volunteers before its planes have been cleared to land.

When I asked Bob how this practice began, he told me about his involvement with the Shoeshine Foundation during the Vietnam War. This foundation was established to adopt and care for the neglected children of American soldiers. Because of their American blood, these children were not accepted in Vietnamese society. Before the war ended, Bob and his friends had adopted over twenty-five hundred of these kids.

On April 23, 1975, a C5A crashed while taking off from Tan Son Nhut. More than four hundred children who were being evacuated to the United States were on board. Many of them were Shoeshine Foundation children. Half were killed immediately. Many others were said to be injured.

When Bob heard of the crash, he called the State Department and asked the status of the relief efforts. "Don't worry," he was told. "We will have a plane there in seventy-two hours."

Macauley reminded the State Department that many of these children were infants. They would not live long without assistance.

Again the response came, "We are doing the best we can."

For most of us a bureaucratic response from an official agency of that size would have been the end of it. For Bob Macauley, it would be just the beginning. He decided to charter a jet to rescue those kids.

"I called Pan Am and asked them what it would cost," Bob recalls, "and they said a quarter of a million, 10 percent down. I told them to put the plane in the air and I would put the check in the mail."

What Bob didn't tell them was that he didn't have the money. "But this all happened on a Friday," he explains. "By the time Pan Am got the check I knew it would be Monday. I figured the kids would be safe by then and we could worry about the rest later."

Sure enough, on Sunday morning, Pan Am called to say the plane was on its way. "They wanted the balance," Bob said, "so I wrote them another rubber check."

When the check bounced, as Bob knew it would, he put his house up as collateral. He remembers coming home to find his wife waiting on the porch. "Bob," she said, "the TV crews were here. What's this about the house?"

When you see that kind of a fearless response, you can't help wondering what makes the difference. How it is possible for some to live so much in the moment. The answer is in Bob's response when I asked him what he would have done if donations had not poured in as they did and covered his debt?

"Anytime I can trade my house for two hundred kids," Bob said, "I'll trade all day long. A house is a material possession. You can get another house."

When you know what your values are all the other decisions are easier.

QUESTION:

Take a moment to think of those around you. Mother Teresa believed, "The very fact that God has placed a certain soul in your way is a sign that God wants you to do something for them." What opportunities do the people near you offer?

II

LOVE YOURSELF

"WE MAY NOT BE GOD, BUT WE ARE OF GOD EVEN AS A LITTLE DROP OF WATER IS OF THE OCEAN."

...*GANDHI*

The Gift
of Your
Misfortune

In the summer of 1989, Diane Cirincione and Jerry Jampolsky took me to visit a friend in a San Francisco hospital. Their friend had contracted AIDS and was dying.

As we talked, this gentle soul led me through the story of his life, describing how he arrived at this place in time. The picture he painted was painful, full of unresolved hurts, a struggle for acceptance and identity. As he described his life, it was clear the most painful scars were caused by rejection and a failure to meet other people's expectations, resulting in an inability to come to terms with himself and find peace.

In contrast, I was struck by the peacefulness and acceptance with which he now greeted the dying process. He spoke of how much he had learned since his infection, about the new understanding he had gained of life, and about the gift of true friends. He said in conclusion, "It was the best thing that has ever happened to me."

I asked him if he really meant what he had just said. He looked at me without hesitation and said, "I wouldn't go back. If I had to choose between being the way I was without AIDS and being the way I am with AIDS – even knowing that I am going to die soon – I wouldn't go back."

He had come to understand life is one piece. There are no dead ends. Our troubles, to paraphrase Henry Ward Beecher, more often than not are only tools by which God fashions us for better things.

No one knows this better than Wally Amos. More than half the population of the United States knows him as "The Cookie Man." Wally opened the first gourmet chocolate chip cookie store in the world and his name became synonymous with chocolate chip cookies. He promoted his image with such success that his trademark-embroidered shirt and Panama hat now reside in the Smithsonian National Museum of American History.

What most people don't know is that Wally has no part of the profits from the products that bear his name and likeness. Most people would find it hard to believe that he lost control of his company to partners and outside investors who quickly became his employers, capitalizing on his name, reputation, and his works of charity.

When Wally decided to start another company, his former partners replied by suing him. They sought an injunction, forcing him to shut down his new company and telling him he would never be allowed to use his legal name in any other business venture.

"I refused to be reduced and defeated," Wally said. "I refused to let them control me." With his characteristic good humor, Wally started another venture he called The Uncle Noname Cookie Company. At the same time, he reorganized his finances and gathered support while he fought to regain his name in court. Within a year, his suit was settled. He regained the right to use his name for any business that did not involve food. He also regained the right to use his name, likeness, and reputation for publicity purposes in marketing his own cookies.

But along the way, Wally had gained a larger, personal victory. "The willingness to grow through one's problems keeps you on the journey toward greatness and happiness," Wally says. "We evolve out of crisis more often than happiness."

When the Soul Comes Alive

"The mark of your ignorance is the depth of your belief in injustice and tragedy. What the caterpillar calls the end of the world, the Master calls a butterfly."

...Richard Bach

Death came into Maryanne Kelly's life when she was twenty. First her neighbor and best friend died suddenly and unexpectedly. Then, a few months later, her husband committed suicide, killing himself with a high-powered rifle in the living room on Mother's Day, leaving her alone and pregnant. The baby she had been carrying lived four days and died.

Two years later, when she was twenty-three, her father died. By the time she was twenty-eight, she had lost a second husband, this time of heart disease. When that happened, Maryanne says, "I truly believed that if I loved you, you would die."

By the time she was thirty, Maryanne had lost eleven people close to her. Over the following years, she sought support anywhere and everywhere. Her priest told her to pray. Her doctor medicated her with sleeping pills and tranquilizers. Her psychiatrist suggested she get her mind off it.

While she struggled with these diverse prescriptions, her nineteen-year-old son, Scott, was severely burned in a freak explosion. He lost both arms and all of his facial structure. The only way Maryanne knew it was her son was because she could see his toes, the only recognizable part of his body.

Maryanne lived in the burn unit with her son for twenty days, all the way to the last beat of his heart. The most difficult part, she said, was not to pray for him to live.

Any doctor will tell you, few things are as painful as a severe burn. She listened to his incredible suffering, saw what little was left of the artistic, gregarious man who had been her son, and could not in her mother's heart will him to live like that.

When it came, the death of her son nearly ended Maryanne's desire to live, but at the same time it awakened a new part of her. "In our sleep," Aeschylus wrote, "pain which cannot forget falls drop by drop upon the heart until, in our own despair, against our will, comes wisdom through the awful grace of God."

"I wrote in my journal every day," Maryanne remembers. "I worked hard on my grief and then one day I realized – maybe this is when the soul comes to life – this is what I am supposed to do. Each of us must, in Mother Teresa's words, learn to love the hole in the heart as much as the heart itself.

"The hole in the heart is the gift of this life. With this life are so many joys, but there is also pain. In fact, one of the only ways we know joy is because of pain. We have to accept it all because it is part of who we are."

Out of Maryanne's pain and her search for support in dealing with death came the Centre for Living with Dying, which she founded to help others with their grief. Beginning with a small group meeting in her living room, the Centre has grown to have provided bereavement support to over 180,000 people.

Maryanne says death has taught her what to value in life. "The two most important things go hand in hand," she says. "We have to learn to love ourselves – we judge ourselves far more harshly than anyone else ever judges us – and we have to come to understand intellectually and emotionally that today is the day of our death. Every day is the day of my death, I just don't know which one.

"You've got to remember life is not a free ride. I feel so sad for people that come to the end of their lives somewhere in their seventies, eighties, or whatever, and find themselves unhappy and remorseful. When you ask them what it is that they wished they had done more of, it isn't shopping. You don't hear people expressing great regret that they didn't buy a bigger home or a better car.

"When you go into a room where people are dying, whether it be a child or an adult, you find out what's most important to us. It's not our material goods, but our relationships. When death comes into our lives, what everyone wishes they had one more chance to do is say I love you, give someone a hug, or say I'm sorry.

"Today is that chance. So, hug more. Touch more. Kiss more. Make love more. Walk near the ocean, hear the sound. Sit on the top of the mountain. Risk opening your heart."

QUESTION:

Every whole heart has been broken. It has been broken and healed, brought together again stronger in the broken places. The gift of the hole in your heart is in the strength it creates when it heals. This is the essence of your humanity, the center of your being. What is the hole in your heart?

L I T T L E   M I R A C L E S

"Good may be accomplished by small degrees, but it is
not thereby rendered small."

...Zeno

When we think of poverty, we tend to think of the inner city,
but you haven't really seen poverty in America until you have
been to Appalachia.

Becky and Bobby Simpson have lived all their lives in what
is left of a mining town that defines poverty. They grew up
"hard" as Bobby would say and, in the process, developed a
feel for the people.

Becky remembers watching her little brother die of pneumonia when she was five. Two years later her sister almost followed him. The house was so cold, it seemed warmer outside.

In 1962, Bobby lost his sight and could no longer get work.
Hard times got harder. "We nearly starved to death," Bobby
remembers. "What we had to live on was what we raised ourselves – garden stuff."

Ultimately, what saved them was an even bigger catastro-
phe. One summer, when it seemed things couldn't get much
worse, the skies opened up. It rained seemingly without end
for days and their valley was hit with a series of floods.

The damage done by the deluge was complicated by the
ecological damage caused by strip mining in the mountains
above them. There soon wasn't a bridge left in the county.

Bobby says, "There were maybe three good cars left in the
whole valley. We lost all of our wells, and the water in our

house was four feet deep." Becky remembers the hopelessness of standing on a crate near the bank of the river crying in frustration. While she cried, the knowledge came to her that she had friends she hadn't met yet.

Acting on that thought, Becky got on the phone and got to work. She organized, cajoled, and testified. She arranged meetings, put together petitions, and testified at hearings. Before she was done, she had obtained $1 million to dredge the silt out of the creek. Then she went to work looking for money for reclamation of the mountains. Surprising even herself, she was able to raise $940,000 to stabilize the mountains and restore their ecological base.

From that success emerged the purpose and direction of their lives. Though they lived on nothing more than Bobby's disability pay, the Simpsons founded the Cranks Creek Survival Center, which sees to those in need in a dozen counties in the tri-state area of Kentucky, Virginia, and Tennessee.

Much of their effort goes to aid their neighbors – people like Franklin Hill who was living in a coal shed until the Simpsons and their volunteers built him a little twelve-by-twenty-four-foot house, and Henry Furman who lived by himself in a pump house, and Michael Taylor who lived in a floorless chicken coop with his fourteen-month-old baby.

In all, the Simpsons have restored more than four hundred houses in the surrounding hills. Thousands of volunteers – Becky's unknown friends – have come to help. They have come from the entire East Coast and more than a dozen foreign nations including India, China, Africa, and Brazil. It is a testimony to the depth of poverty in Appalachia that residents of countries we tend to think so poor would travel halfway around the world to aid Americans who are even poorer.

Bobby supervises the building projects and directs the gathering of supplies. He has learned the highways by heart, navigating his driver with a collection of audio and visual cues he has stored up in his mind. "A lot of handicapped people just sit down and don't try to do nothing," he explains, "but there is always something you can do if you try."

While decent housing is the greatest need, the Simpsons also provide clothing, food, and financial assistance. Bobby says it follows the seasons. "Beginning the first of the year, people come by to get garden seeds, fertilizer, and stuff. Then school starts and people are hunting for school clothing, shoes, sweaters. Gets fall and everybody starts hunting something to stay warm. Then it's Thanksgiving time."

At Thanksgiving last year, the Simpsons provided dinner for over 330 families. Christmas is a repeat performance on a larger scale. On average they feed 700 people every Christmas – most of them coal miners who have been laid off and are out of work.

"Whatever someone needs, we try to do," Becky says. "It's like a little miracle. It pleases me to death to be able to help someone else. I had a dream since I was a child that someday I was going to help needy people and now I can do it. If I hear of somebody out of food, I can take them food. Most of the time, I can find them pretty good clothing in here, bed clothes, whatever they need. It has to be a miracle. That's the only way I can explain it."

"If we hadn't started doing this, I'd be dead and gone," Bobby adds. "There's too many people out there that need help. I just couldn't give up. If you can love people good enough, you kind of forget yourself and your problems in helping them."

"Somebody once said it was my work," Becky concludes. "I said, no, it ain't my work. It's my life."

QUESTIONS:

Do you have friends you haven't met yet? Who might they be? Who cares about what you care about?

THE EYE OF THE HEART

"It is only with the heart that one can see rightly; what is essential is invisible to the eye."

...Antoine St. Exupery

Tommie Lee Williams is blind and old enough to be my father. He provided me with the hospitality of his house and treated me with nothing but kindness. Yet I could not resist provoking him.

"How is it," I asked him, "that you are on the giving rather than the receiving end? How can you be taking care of this community when most people would say the community should be taking care of you?"

He sat very still for a moment. Then he leaned forward and softly asked me what I meant.

I knew I was about to make him mad. "Well, you're blind," I said. "Most people would consider that a significant handicap."

His face clouded and his fist came down on the kitchen table between us. "I am not handicapped!" he thundered. He then proceeded to make his point with some agitation.

"You would be surprised at what I can do," he said. "A guy called me and said he heard I still did a little plumbing work. He had a stove that wasn't working right. The top burners weren't catching and the oven wouldn't burn high. He was thinking of getting a new one.

"I said let me look at it. I went down there and regulated the two top burners to let a little more gas in. I could hear what was wrong with it, because if you have too much air coming in with the gas mixture it makes a blowing noise. If it was making a calm noise, I would call a sighted person and ask them to look at the blaze. If it is burning blue, it's okay. So I saved that man from buying a new stove.

"I ran the gas, the water, sewage, everything, from the street to my house. I can hook up heaters or a hot water tank." Tommie Lee went on to describe a house he had recently repaired for a widow, tearing out portions of the back and sides where the siding was bad. Then he installed insulation and cut replacement siding to fit. He said he used a piece of string to measure the hole, and a carpenter's ruler notched with a hacksaw to cut the lumber, and the rest was easy.

Born in Vicksburg to poor, black sharecroppers, Tommie Lee hasn't had it easy. But there is no element of complaint or self-pity in his voice. Rather, there is the pride of the self-reliant. Somehow, they had always gotten by. Somehow, there was always enough to share.

"There were always plenty of eggs, milk, and butter on the farm," Tommie Lee remembers. "My mother would tell me to take these things to someone else's house that had a lot of children. Sweet potatoes, vegetables – we had plenty and we would just give them to other people."

After being a successful plumber for twenty-one years, Tommie Lee woke up one Sunday morning to a series of explosions in his eyes. "You've seen those atomic bombs that they dropped in Nevada," he says, "that's what it was like. There'd be a little straight stream going up and then after it got so high it would mushroom out." He later learned his eyes had hemorrhaged and filled with blood.

Three years after he lost his sight, Tommie Lee started "We Care – Community Services." That was a quarter of a century ago. Since then, he has spent all his time giving away clothes, repairing homes, paying utility bills, and educating kids and, as a result, is strangely thankful for his loss of sight.

"I believe if I could have been able to keep seeing I would not be helping people on as large a scale as I am," Tommie Lee says. "I feel God has wanted me to do this. Because Tommie Lee Williams don't have anything to help anybody with. Everything that comes through this office came from somewhere else.

"When people come into my office and say 'I can't do this,' or 'I can't do that,' and putting up all kinds of excuses, I don't accept that," he says firmly. "I've learned that you can do whatever you want to do and be whatever you want to be. You can be good or you can be bad. You can hurt or you can help. It don't take no degrees.

"It's nice to have degrees, but if you've got a lot of big

degrees and have no mercy or sympathy in your heart and concern for the less fortunate, your degrees aren't worth much. You need to look for ways to help a person out, to make his life better."

Tommie Lee Williams may be blind, but he has great vision. He sees with the eye of the heart.

QUESTIONS:

Tommie Lee is grateful for his misfortune. He feels it enabled him to do what he is doing and has made him a better person. Can you say the same? How have you evolved out of crisis?

WHAT MATTERS?

"The course of human history is determined not by what happens in the skies but what takes place in our hearts."

...*Sir Arthur Keith*

On March 29, 1978, Richard Bloch, cofounder of H&R Block, was told to get his affairs in order.

"I was young and vibrant – at the top of the world," Dick remembers. "I had gone to see my physician because I had a sore arm. My worst complaint was that I couldn't hold a tennis racket. The next thing I knew, I was dying of cancer.

"I was stunned. I asked, 'Is there anywhere else I can go?' And he said, 'I will send you anywhere you want to go, but I guarantee you we know everything there is to know about this. There is nothing we can do.'"

"Nothing I have ever gone through was as bad," Dick says. "A human being cannot live without hope."

After five days of agony, Bloch decided he wasn't ready to quit. With his wife's support, he sought another opinion and found a doctor who confirmed the diagnosis but promised a cure. "You are a very sick boy," the doctor said. "But we are going to cure you so you can work for cancer."

The doctor was as good as his word. Two years later, Richard Bloch went home cured.

"I realized I owed a huge debt," Dick says. "I knew money wasn't the answer. Compared with what the government gives, anything else is a token. I knew I didn't know enough about the cause of cancer or the treatment of cancer to be helpful. But I did know something about fighting cancer. This is my field of expertise and this is where I went to work."

Bloch was born an entrepreneur. His first enterprise started at the age of nine when he found a printing press in his uncle's attic. By his twelfth birthday, he owned three automatic presses and was doing the printing for all the high schools in Kansas City. He was making so much money by the time he left high school that he didn't want to quit to go to college.

At his father's insistence, he sold the printing business. He went on to attend the Wharton School of Finance where he started another business – buying and selling remodeled cars. Then in 1955, after a short stint with a brokerage house, Dick joined with his brother, Henry, in the company that came to be known as H&R Block.

After his bout with cancer, Dick's entire life changed. He resigned his position as chairman of H&R Block. He started a cancer hot line, established a cancer support center at the University of Missouri, and designed a computer program to improve the treatment of cancer patients by making the latest research and treatment protocols instantly available to all.

"Half of what the doctors who graduated ten years ago were told was untreatable can now be treated," Bloch says. "We identified every possible kind of treatment for every kind of cancer – over eight hundred – and put them in a giant computer so every doctor in the country can have access to the latest information. People are dying not because treatment isn't there, but because the doctor treating the specific patient doesn't know about it."

Bloch's efforts were so successful that the National Cancer Institute adopted this program in 1984. NCI estimated at that time that more than forty thousand lives a year would be saved as a result.

"My goal is very narrow," Dick says. "I want to help the next person who gets cancer get the very best possible treatment. I know that's not the most important thing. I would find a cure for cancer if I could. But this is where we have some expertise and where we can be constructive."

Bloch provides all the resources for his crusade personally, with the exception of office space provided by H&R Block. He is in the office every morning between 4:30 and 5 A.M., much earlier than he ever came in when he was in business. "That's because the rewards are far greater," he says. "Saving just one life makes it all worthwhile."

As his brother Henry noted, "Dick will talk with anyone with cancer any time, at home or at the office, because he wants to help."

"I owe a huge debt," Dick explains. "I still wonder what more can I do to repay that debt? If a few minutes of my time will help someone, that's the least I can do."

QUESTION:

One of the fundamental challenges of life is to discover what matters to you. Dick Bloch gave up his life in business to help other people fight against cancer. What do you want to be your life's work?

BELIEVING IN THE POWER OF LOVE

"It is my firm belief that it is love that sustains the earth. There is only life where there is love."

...Gandhi

What is the one indispensable ingredient of life? What is the gift of God and how is God manifested in this world? What is the only way one person can positively influence another? Where will we find at once the solution to the problems in our lives and the problems of the world?

Ask Bob Macauley, who in the last decade has generated more than $2 billion worth of aid to those in need, or Mimi Silbert, who has done the equally impossible and rehabilitated more than eighteen thousand felons most people said were incorrigible. Ask Lois Lee who has made it her life's work to reclaim the children of the night, or the banker, Hugh Jones, who received his greatest dividend when he found his life transformed by the gesture of a child from a distant land.

It is as Mother Teresa has said. We were created out of love to love and be loved. It is love that acts. In the words of Bob Macauley, "There is no other hope."

THE SKY'S THE LIMIT

"Each man has inside him a basic decency and goodness. If he listens to it and acts on it, he is giving a
great deal of what the world needs most."

...Pablo Casals

After living without heat and light for two months and being
unable to feed her children, Bea Gaddy resorted to prayer.

She said, "I asked the Supreme Being to show me how to take
care of *my* children. I did not ask for anybody else's children. I
just wanted to know how to feed my children and myself."

Bea has been homeless most of her life. Her strongest
memory is of always being hungry.

"As children, we used to fight at the garbage cans," she
recalls. "We all did it – my brothers and myself. Other families.

"It is degrading. It is very dehumanizing. But you don't
think about that if you're a child and you're hungry. You go
into that can and get that food, wash it off and use it. You
don't thinking about it, because not a soul is saying, 'Why you
in that can? Let me show you a better way.' You've got to find
your own way to come out of that can."

As an adult, most of Bea's time was spent sitting and
"waiting for a welfare check." Then in the early '60s, after
she was evicted from her apartment in Brooklyn, she moved
to Baltimore to be near a friend. "I was living in Patterson
Park. I was getting food stamps," she remembers, "but I still
couldn't feed my children or pay the rent."

The prayer came out of her desperation and with it Bea sent a promise – "Show me how to do these things and I promise I will forever give back," she said. "I will walk with the people. I will do whatever I have to do to make people stop sitting and feeling sorry for themselves."

With a flash of inspiration that came after her prayer, she asked her pastor if she could borrow a garbage can that had wheels. While her neighbors watched through drawn curtains she wheeled it up to the corner store.

Somehow, she said, she found the courage to ask the owner, "Would you please give me the food that you are going to throw away tonight?"

The owner looked at her strangely, Bea remembers. "I thought the man was going to say, 'Get out of my store,' but he didn't. He asked me why I wanted it and when I said, 'So we can eat it,' he practically filled this huge can up before I came out of the store."

At a second store the owner finished filling the can. Encouraged by her success, Bea emptied the can at home and went to a third store down the street.

"This man actually filled up the whole garbage can with food," Bea remembers. "When I came home this time, everybody came out on the street and I said there's no stopping us now."

Very quickly from there, she says, she came up with the idea of opening an emergency food center. "I might have started out for selfish reasons, but I soon realized I had enough food not only for my children but for other women who were eating out of the garbage can just like I did."

From food, Bea moved to shelter. Then she broadened her focus to provide whatever people needed. "If people need a place to stay and they are not a threat to themselves or anyone else, I will make space for them," she says now.

Bea sleeps in the basement of her own home and renovates four homes at a time for her neighbors to use. When she looks back at it, she says, the hardest part was learning to believe in herself.

"If you don't have self-worth, if you don't have respect for yourself, how can you respect anyone else," she says. "I had to learn that I had a brain, because I had been told I was no good and never going to amount to anything. Then, I had to learn to use it.

"Now, I wonder why in the name of God I sat waiting all those years. Once you learn to love yourself the sky's the limit."

QUESTIONS:

What are you waiting for? Is there a need you see or a concern you carry? What are you doing about it?

SERVING TIME

"We must learn to love each other or die."

...W. H. Auden

"Our average resident is violent, belongs to a gang, has eighteen felony convictions," Mimi Silbert says. "That means eighteen strikes in a country where three strikes puts you in prison for life. And we have never had an arrest. We have never had a crime committed in twenty-five years by these people."

Mimi runs the Delancey Street Foundation in San Francisco. She has helped turn around more than eighteen thousand hardened criminals, making productive citizens of former felons, drug addicts, and prostitutes.

Mimi's program evolved out of her experience as a prison psychologist a quarter of a century ago. She quickly decided that the system of institutionalization and punishment didn't work.

"It doesn't take a long time in the field to realize that one of the horrors is that the people on the bottom are the receivers, and nothing but the receivers. They are either receivers of punishment and hate and aggression, or they are the receivers of welfare, the receivers of therapy.

"But they are never the doers. They are never the givers. And it's those of us who are givers who get to feel terrific about ourselves."

From the beginning, Mimi's goal was to create a criminal rehabilitation center with a central tenet of self-sufficiency. She started out in a small San Francisco apartment. She worked with ex-cons and drug addicts, holding group counseling sessions and seeking training for them in employable skills. Everyone involved, including Silbert, pooled their incomes and shared resources.

Today, Delancey Street Foundation is housed on the waterfront in a thirty-million-dollar, three-acre complex called the Embarcadero Triangle, complete with shops, restaurants, and theaters. The complex, funded by an unsecured bank loan, was built entirely by Silbert's extended brood of ex-cons while she personally supervised the job.

Silbert is the only nonresident employee of Delancey Street. The operation is staffed and run entirely by ex-cons and earns about $6 million a year. Among the business the residents operate are retail stores, a restaurant, a moving company, and a million-dollar Christmas tree sale project.

Despite Delancey Street's phenomenal growth and success over the years, the basic tenets that Silbert began with remain constant: Each resident must own up to self-responsibility, develop at least three marketable skills, earn a high school equivalency degree, perform volunteer work, and serve as a role model for other residents. "Each one teach one" is the guiding principle of Delancey Street.

"We compare ourselves to Harvard. Both are four-year programs. They take the top 2 percent and teach them everything they need to know to become successful. We take the bottom 2 percent of the population – we're equally snotty about our bottom 2 percent – and then we teach people who are used to being self-centered and full of hate to become full of love and take care of each other. In the need to help, all your strengths will emerge."

QUESTIONS:

All of the people at the bottom of the ladder, as Mimi observes, are receivers. Others are providing for and taking care of them economically and spiritually. By this measure, where are you? How far up the ladder have you climbed?

L O V E   I S   T H E   B R I D G E

"Love is all we have, the only way each can help the other."

...Euripides

In October 1983, Hugh Jones was made chairman and CEO of Barnett Bank of Jacksonville. About a year later, the son of a friend died after an unsuccessful heart surgery.

Looking for a way to help channel his friend's grief and to draw something positive out of this negative experience, Hugh began investigating the possibility of establishing a memorial heart program that would benefit other kids in need. When he learned there was no real need for such a program in the United States, his thoughts turned to Korea. A veteran of the Korean War, Hugh knew thousands of Korean children were in need of heart surgery.

"The first children arrived in March 1985 with great fanfare – a seven-year-old boy and a six-year-old girl, named Young Joo Yoo," Hugh remembers. "I still have vivid memories of carrying the little girl off the plane, finally getting them both in the car to drive to my house, some thirty-five miles from the airport. My wife and I had no earthly idea how we would communicate with them, but we were told not to worry.

"Sure enough, with a combination of drawing pictures and pointing, we were able to settle them in and make them comfortable. Finally, on a Saturday night I had to take Yoo to University Hospital. She was expected to go into surgery on Monday morning.

"I think I was more scared than the little girl that something would happen in surgery. I could not sleep at all that night. At about 4 A.M., I simply got in my car and went to the hospital to sit by my little girl.

"As the nurses came to take her to the operating room, I saw for the first time tears in her eyes and then I think a miracle happened. She turned around and lifted her arms up to me as though she thought I would be able to get her through that surgery. I also had tears in my eyes when I picked her up. Instead of her going down to the operating room in a mobile stretcher, I carried her there. We hugged each other as tightly as we could all the way.

"Those three or four minutes changed my life. There was a cultural difference between us, a language difference, a color difference, and a heck of an age difference, but in those few precious moments I realized none of that mattered. All that can be surmounted – if there is love."

Over the next ten years Hugh and his friends were able to provide life-saving surgery to seventy children. With a little persuasion, local hospitals agreed to perform the surgeries. The airlines agreed to provide transportation, and friends on both ends of the bridge agreed to help make the necessary arrangements and provide support.

At the same time, Hugh established an unprecedented bankwide employee volunteer program called the Community Involvement Initiative. Under Hugh's direction, all the bank's employees were asked to put something back into the community through volunteer programs of their own design.

Hugh's initiative led Barnett's employees to contribute over forty thousand hours of effort a year to community projects.

Hugh personally took the lead in establishing a Ronald McDonald House. He also cochaired the city's children's campaign, helped build houses for Habitat for Humanity, and was a pillar of the local United Way.

Hugh retired from the bank two years ago, but his community involvement continues. He has become heavily involved with a local hospice, helps send terminally ill children to DisneyWorld, and last year he took the lead in establishing a homeless shelter for the city of Jacksonville.

"That little girl taught me the most important lesson of my life," Hugh said. "I only regret I didn't learn it earlier. Up to the time I was fifty years old, I worked hard and focused on doing well for the bank, our clients, and myself. I measured progress by the investments I made and the income we received. Now what's important to me is 'psychic income' – the feeling that I get when I know I can make a difference in someone's life."

QUESTIONS:

The thing we call the soul, ancient Greeks named the psyche. For them it was the animating force of the universe, the life force that governed and sustained all things. What gives you "psychic income"? How can you multiply the experiences that feed your soul?

Unconditional Love

"The ultimate lesson all of us have to learn is unconditional love — not only for others but ourselves as
well."

...Elisabeth Kubler-Ross

"Basically, I just dare anyone to mess with my kids," says Lois
Lee. When she says "anyone" there's a firmness to her mouth
and a glint in her eye that tells you she means it. Lois will take
on *anyone* – pimps and politicians, cops and madams – to protect her kids.

Lois Lee knows more about teen prostitutes and prostitution than anyone in the country. Her interest began with a
graduate school research project at UCLA. As she got to know
the girls, some of the older ones (a girl of eighteen is a veteran
on the streets) said it's really too late for us, but you've got to
do something about the kids.

"I'd meet these kids on the street and say, 'if you ever need
anything, call me,'" Lois said. To her surprise they did. Over
the next three years more than 250 kids came through her
house.

"Some of them thought as soon as I finished my dissertation
I would put them back on the streets like everyone else. And I
said, 'no, I'll set up a program for you,'" she recalls. That program became known as Children of the Night and is located
on the outskirts of Hollywood.

Before I met Lois and visited her place I had an opinion of

prostitutes probably shared by millions of Americans. My judgments were colored by questions of morality, perceptions of greed, laziness, and lack of self-respect.

Prostitutes were sleazy people I passed with discomfort in a tacky part of town on my way somewhere else. I half-believed those who said that prostitution is a victimless crime. After all, no one was forcing anyone to do anything. It was just another economic exchange – time for money.

If you see Lois's kids, this economic analysis is hard to sustain. Her kids have been abused and victimized at every level of our society. Most of them were sexually abused as small children.

"They are raped," Lois says. "They are beaten and cut up, sodomized. They are subjected to AIDS and everything else you can imagine. There is nothing victimless about it. People just don't go out on the streets and say, 'gee, I think I'll be a prostitute today.'"

It is more than just a personal transaction between two strangers. It is an immense problem that nobody wants to talk about and everyone wants to cover up. Each year, about a million and a half children run away from home. A third of these, by a conservative estimate, get involved in some kind of prostitution or have a brush with pornography.

The solution, Lois says, is unconditional love. "We don't punish them. We are there for them, regardless of the choices they make. If they want our help, we are here for them. And if they want to go back on the streets, we understand that they have their reasons and they know we are still here for them.

"We don't have any magic wand," Lois answered. "We don't do any therapy here. But if you ask any kid I've worked with at any stage of the game, they will tell you 'I turned around because she's there for me, because she loves me, because she is my mom.' It's just the basics. It's one, two, three."

So far, the ones and twos have added up to more than eight thousand kids Lois has helped escape a life on the streets.

Lois's message is that love is not love if it comes with conditions, claims, or controls, and she reminds us we are no different. Much of what most of us do, we do for love. We live with the illusion that we can buy love with good behavior, good grades, good jobs, pretty things, success, and money. Often, we become what our parents want us to become, do what our children want us to do, with the illusion that they will love us ever more.

Like Lois's kids, we must learn that love can never be bought. Love is the gift of a willing heart or it is nothing.

QUESTIONS:

Love, to be real, must be unconditional. Conditional love is a manifestation of the ego and reflects a desire to control. Who do you love unconditionally? Do they know that? Are your actions toward them telling them something else? Is your message of love being lost in your criticism and diluted by your desire to control their behavior?

HAVING REVERENCE FOR LIFE

Can you love the Creator and not respect all his creations?

God's gifts are in man's hands. What we do to each other, we do to ourselves. What we do to the land, we do to our legacy. We have not inherited the earth. We hold it in trust for our children. Some day we must deliver. Some day we must answer.

MOTHER TERESA'S ORANGE

"When I die, I should be ashamed to leave enough to build me a monument if there were a wanting friend above ground."

...Alexander Pope

One day in May, after twelve years of dreaming of meeting Mother Teresa, Jessica Davey found herself on a plane to India. A week before, she had been finishing a paper at college, now she was on her way to Delhi, scared out of her mind.

Jessica left for Calcutta without an invitation, without a friend, without any sense of what she would find. All she had was her dream and a plan. She would find a place to stay and then knock on Mother Teresa's door.

Over the next few months, Jessica spent time in three of Mother Teresa's fifteen homes in Calcutta, and in her community for leprosy patients, but most of her time was spent at Prem Dam, Mother Teresa's home for mentally ill, handicapped, and tuberculosis patients. She worked alongside the sisters and other volunteers as they cared for the 350 destitute patients living there.

Her days began at 5:45 A.M. with mass in Mother's house. Then came breakfast. By 8 A.M. she was at work. Her days ended at 6 P.M. with adoration and reflection. She lived with a small community of volunteers at the Salvation Army dormitories.

"When you walk back to the dorm at night you are confronted by the fact that the beggars have not retreated indoors," Jessica wrote. "The mothers and their babies have no shelter or food. You must be careful after dark not to step on anybody. You have to realize you are always walking through someone's living room. It's shocking to realize people spend their entire lives in and on the streets.

"In Calcutta, the pavement dwellers arise around 5 A.M. Those that wake go about their days; those that don't lie there until someone cares enough to remove the body. For a while, I didn't realize some of the people I was stepping over were dead."

Because resources are so scarce, Jessica noted how careful the sisters were about conservation. "Today, we needed more washing powder," she wrote in her journal. "Sister sent me into the supply closet for a sack which I emptied carefully, shaking the last bits out into the can. Sister Columbia reminded me to wash the sack with the clothes, to be sure we used every granule of washing powder. Then the burlap sack would be used for making pillows. Tiny bits of soap are saved, melted down, and used again. Nothing is wasted, absolutely nothing."

Jessica began finding herself wondering, "How can I avoid being wasteful? How can I re-enter a developed country and culture and not get wrapped up in its excesses?

"I expected to be overwhelmed in India. I expected to find deep truths revealed in big ways. However, today a half-eaten orange was significant to me. As I was eating it, I realized that I didn't want it any more. Then this half-eaten orange became a burden to me. I knew it would be a feast for a street kid living not more than ten steps from my bed.

"Mother says, 'You and I, we create poverty because we do not share.' I never realized how much I waste. I hope every time I order dinner or turn on the water, I can remember that half-eaten orange and see a street child's outstretched hand.

"The hunger of Calcutta is overwhelming but it is first and foremost a physical hunger. The poverty of my culture is a personal, spiritual hunger. Mother talks about this hunger all the time. I see it too, now. We isolate ourselves. One reinforces the other because we don't share. We don't share our food and our resources. We don't share ourselves.

"Calcutta made me feel so small, yet at the same time, I have never been so empowered. Every little bit here helps. Anyone can make a difference, a big difference to one person. Yet, for every outstretched hand you touch, there are hundreds more."

QUESTIONS:

Jessica Davey resolved after visiting Mother Teresa that she would not get wrapped up in the world's excesses. How can you change your life to limit what you waste? What do you have that you can share with someone in need?

S E P A R A T E N E S S

"The word 'hell' is from the old English, meaning to separate, to build a wall around. To be 'helled' was to be shut off from."

....Ralph Waldo Trine

When Reverend Steinbruck arrived at Luther Place, he found a church surrounded by brothels, palm readers, and drug dealers. "It made Sodom and Gomorrah look like a Sunday school picnic," he recalls. "No X-rated movie could do it justice. One Saturday night, *The Washington Post* counted three hundred hookers within a block of this place."

The leadership felt something had to be done about all this to protect the church and its congregation from the people on the street. Rev. Steinbruck's response was to make the street people his congregation.

"All people are God's people," he explained, "not just church people. Too many church people are too isolated and remote, locked up behind stained glass windows. They don't know what's happening, while people are dying every night on the streets."

Steinbruck began by sending out a call to action. He wrote one thousand letters to congregations and social service organizations in and around Washington asking for help, but he got no response. The city had yet to recognize what was soon to be a national crisis.

Given the lack of response, Rev. Steinbruck did the only

thing he could do. He appealed to the leadership of Luther Place and obtained permission to open the doors of the church to the poor and homeless.

"I believe that congregations ought to take responsibility for their community and be deeply involved, immersed, plunged into the problems of their neighborhood. Not simply worry about whether their roof is leaking or their organ is off-key," Steinbruck says.

"That first winter, the emergency shelter was located in our social hall. From the moment we welcomed our first homeless into that makeshift shelter, we had a new reason for being – namely refuge.

"Within twenty-four hours, the word had gotten out and the church was filled to capacity," Steinbruck remembers. "People came in from everywhere, carrying their bags and all their possessions with them."

The N Street Village, as Steinbruck's refuge is now called, has operated twenty-four hours a day, 365 days a year, for over twenty-two years. It provides a safe haven and a healing place for the homeless and a loving pathway designed to take the addicted from hopelessness to independence.

"We take great pride in saying to those for whom there is no room in the inn, no other place, you've got Luther Place," Steinbruck says. "If somebody knocks at that door at three o'clock in the morning, some woman who has no place and is endangered either from the weather elements or other elements on the street, this innkeeper better have a bloody good answer to the Householder who one day is going to ask for an account of my watch here at Luther Place. And you don't have to go five years to the seminary to know the appropriate theological response to a knock on the door. You open it."

Classical physics rested on a vision of the separateness of things, but the foundation of modern science is the sense that everything is related. Experiment after experiment shows us how things influence each other across the boundaries of our seeming separateness.

In the same fashion, none of us exists independently of our relationships with each other. We cannot work for the destruction of our neighbor and the exploitation of the weak without damaging our own souls. We cannot act like assassins all day and confine our faith to the weekends, our kindness to our kin. What we do at work comes home with us. What we do all day, we are all night.

It is this sense of the wholeness of things that Steinbruck has brought to his church. "That is why this church is engaged with the world," he says. "That is why we deal with the front page, not just the religious page. What happens in Bosnia is a religious issue. Homelessness is a religious question."

Steinbruck reminds us it is not enough to love our families and our own homes. We must also love those around us who are different, all those who seem strange, all the outcasts. "Everybody is wanted. Everybody is needed," he concludes. "There is a place and a purpose for everybody. We just have to look and see the value intrinsic in each person."

The cost of our indifference, the nature of our loss if we fail was calculated by President Truman. "Men, all men, belong to each other," Truman said, "and he who shuts himself away diminishes himself, and he who shuts another away from him destroys himself."

QUESTIONS:

Rev. Steinbruck finds hell in separation. How many walls have you built around yourself? What separates you from your neighbors, your community, and your family? How many places have you created where they cannot go?

THE DANCE

"The world is God's language to us."

...*Simone Weil*

If, as it is said, every man over the age of forty is responsible for his face, Fred Matser has done well. He is a joyful man with sparkling eyes and a ready smile.

At an early age, his father's severe illness forced Fred to take over the responsibility for the family business – a real estate company in The Netherlands. Within ten years he made that company so successful he was able to leave the management in other hands and pursue his own interests.

From the beginning, Fred recalls he had a burning desire to be of service to mankind. He has now established a dozen foundations and is involved in good works on all five continents. One of his many activities is to support the only children's hospital in Brazil, which serves thousands of sick children every week. He also supports everything from a cancer institute in Europe and a dairy farm in India to orphanages in Bangladesh, Tokyo, Sri Lanka, Ethiopia, and Lebanon and an AIDS programs in Russia and Romania.

In his mind, all of his activities are designed to restore the balance between man and his environment. "I want to work to promote harmony," Fred said, "harmony within men, harmony between man and his environment, and harmony between people."

Matser believes the disorder and destruction of the environment is a reflection of the disorder in our minds and hearts. "The damage we do to the world cannot be separated from the damage we do to ourselves," he says.

Over a hundred years ago, Chief Seattle said it this way: "This we know. The earth does not belong to people; people belong to the earth. All things are connected like the blood which unites one family. Whatever befalls the earth befalls the children of the earth. We did not weave the web of life; we are merely a strand in it. Whatever we do to the web, we do to ourselves."

For Fred, this means acting in concert with nature and participating in what Einstein called the dance of the universe. "You can visualize the flow of the universe," Fred says, "by thinking of life as a dance of harmonious patterns of colors or light. Dysfunctional, counterproductive thoughts run against the flow. They are destructive to laws of nature. Functional thoughts, positive actions are in tune and harmonious. We are part of creation and the Creator. We must learn to think with the whole body and tune in to the wisdom of the universe.

"If we are of God, we are part of everything God created," Fred concludes. "In destroying the universe, in disturbing the balance of nature, in separating ourselves from all else that lives, we risk more than we know."

QUESTION:
Are you in harmony with the rhythm of the universe?

THE GIFT OF THE FOREST

"As soon as man began considering himself the highest meaning in the world and the measure of everything, the world began to lose its human dimension and man began to lose control of it."

...Vaclav Havel

Jane Goodall's vision began to form at the age of five when she hid in a chicken coop to see if she could discover "where on a chicken was there an opening big enough for an egg to come out."

She still recalls tumbling out of the hen house in excitement to tell her mother of her discovery. Shortly thereafter – by the age of eight – she had fallen in love with Tarzan and decided she wanted to live in Africa.

"When I was young," she remembers, "I knew that, somehow, I would go to Africa and live with the animals. I don't think I spent too much time wondering exactly how I would do it. I just felt sure the right opportunity would somehow come."

At the age of twenty-three, her dream came true. She was invited to visit a friend whose family had just bought a farm in Kenya. After two months there, she met the man who, more than anyone else, shaped her life – Louis Leakey. The renowned anthropologist offered her a job on the spot, at first working as his secretary, then in the fields of Olduvai Gorge.

But Jane wanted one thing more. She wanted to find a way to watch wild animals living undisturbed lives. She wanted to bridge the distance between man and beast and move among them without fear. She wanted to return to the hen house and discover the secrets of the natural world by observation.

She was twenty-six when she first set foot on Gombe National Park. We met in Washington on her sixty-second birthday and we talked of the gift of the forest and what the animals have taught her.

"Chimpanzees are so like us," she said. "Their blood and their response to disease are like ours. Their brains are more like ours than any other living creature. A lot of their behavior is like ours. They learn by watching one another, then imitating."

If you ask her how close the connection is between us, Jane will tell you that "the line between chimp and human is not clean. It is fuzzy. Chimps do lots of things we like to think of as human. Most important, they feel pain, sorrow, and fear."

The correlation between chimp and man, and the nature of our responsibility, is illustrated by the story of a chimpanzee called Old Man. He had been bought by a zoo in North

America when he was an adolescent. "We still don't know what happened to him in America," Jane said. "But whatever it was, he came to hate people."

Old Man was put on an island with three females. A young man named Marc Casano was given the job of looking after them. He was told how dangerous they were and instructed not to go on the island with the chimps' food. Instead, he paddled a boat until he was close enough to throw the food on the shore.

But as he watched the animals and saw how affectionate they were with each other, he decided he wanted to have a better relationship with them. So he began to make friends. He came closer and closer, until he could actually hand Old Man a banana.

That began their friendship. Soon the two were playing together and Old Man would even let Marc groom him.

One day, Marc slipped and fell, startling an infant nearby. The mother heard the cry and charged protectively, leaping on Marc's back and beginning to bite his neck. Before he could get up, the other two females began to join the attack. He felt his arm go numb and the blood run down his neck. Then he looked up to see Old Man charging at him.

But instead of joining the attack and finishing him off as Marc feared, Old Man seized the females, pulling them off and hurling them away. He stayed close by as Marc dragged himself to the boat, threatening the females every time they tried to attack again.

"Old Man saved Marc's life," Jane said. "I tell that story often because it has taught me a lot. If a chimpanzee can reach out to help a human, then surely humans can reach out and try to help chimps and all the other living creatures we live with in the world today."

Goodall's understanding of nature and her resulting reverence for life has led her to campaign for compassion. The woman who yearned for the jungle at the age of eight and spent thirty-six years living in solitude and solidarity with wild animals now lives on airplanes, is immersed in civilization and travels constantly – never spending more than two weeks in one place.

"I hate my suitcases, packing, unpacking. Ironing – I hate ironing," she says. "But it is all made worthwhile when I think of the forest and what it has given me. It makes me sad that I can only get there for such short visits. But then I think of how lucky I have been. I have spent years doing what I wanted to do most of all – being with wild, free chimpanzees in the forest. Now is my paying back time."

Jane Goodall reminds us that caring is seamless. It is not one thing to save man and another to save the animals. "Together," she says, "we can make the world a better place for all living things." If we are to survive, we must learn to love the animals and the whole world with an all-embracing love.

QUESTIONS:

Jane Goodall developed a vision for herself at an early age. She knew she wanted to go to Africa and study wild animals. What was your childhood vision of yourself? Are you living that vision or is it still a dream?

SEEING
YOURSELF IN
OTHERS

Early last year, Rachel Rossow called
in some excitement. "I've got it," she
said.

From the time we first met, Rachel
and I had noted a strange, inexplica-
ble kinship. We had often remarked
on the closeness we felt and struggled for an explanation. It is a feeling most people have had, seeing in
a stranger a familiarity they cannot
explain.

It happened when I went to greet
Fred Matser at the airport in
Baltimore in 1989. I had only the
roughest of descriptions – age and
coloring. He could have been any of
a dozen people coming out of cus-
toms. But with no description of me
at all, Fred came toward me as I
moved toward him. We knew each
other instantly. As we talked, we
found ourselves connecting on so
many levels it was unsettling. It was
as if we were brothers who had suddenly found and recognized each
other. We adopted each other on the
spot to formalize our feelings.

Fred lives in Holland, thousands of

miles and six time zones away, but all I have to do is think of him and he will call and vice versa.

The first time this happened, I was startled. My wife and I were talking about Fred on the way home from church. I was wondering how he was and thought I would give him a call that afternoon. Within half an hour Fred called for no apparent reason. He said he had been thinking of me.

The same thing happens all the time with Rachel, Hugh Jones, and other members of my extended family. Mysteriously, I seem to know when they are troubled or going through a difficult period – and they me.

This now happens often enough that I have begun to take it for granted. I had given up any hope of finding an explanation when Rachel called to offer one.

She said she had started reading a new book that morning and couldn't get past the first line. "I read it over and over until I had to call," she said. "This is it: 'There is no distance between souls.'

"That's exactly the way I feel," she concluded. "It is like we are connected no matter how far apart we are."

Rachel is right. All humanity is indivisible but some connections are stronger, more immediate, more vivid. There truly are kindred spirits. You know when you have found your soul mate, as I have in my dear wife, Angela. You know when you meet soul sisters and brothers. With some the bond of brotherhood is so strong, every time you meet is like coming home.

C O M P A S S I O N

"The purpose of life is to serve – to show compassion
and the will to help others."

...Albert Schweitzer

Father Mac is a fanatical White Sox fan. For his golden jubilee, he wanted the recessional hymn to be "Take Me Out to the Ball Game." His car carries the plate "Sox1" and his language is peppered with baseball metaphors.

"My goal is to move somebody else along the base paths of life," he says. "That's my objective, to move some needy person along the base paths of life to the home plate of God's friendship.

"Life itself is a ball game," he says. "It's hits, runs, and errors, strikeouts and sacrifices. I think we are always looking at home runs instead of sacrificing ourselves."

Father Mac is more formally known as Father Ignatius McDermott. For fifty years he has worked with those we now call alcoholics, those on what we used to call "skid row."

"Skid row to me is not a piece of real estate," Father Mac says. "It's a state of mind. I found more people dependent upon alcohol or chemicals residing in a penthouse than in a flophouse."

When Father Mac began his crusade against drink, there was no such thing as alcoholism. Those who overimbibed were thought of as lazy and weak. They were considered derelicts and bums who lacked willpower and social responsibility.

"I always felt the alcoholic was a sick person, socially,

emotionally, mentally, and physically," Father Mac responds. "Most of them didn't even know they were drinking. They didn't know they were sick."

The best testament to Father Mac's success is that the rest of society now shares his opinion. Chicago is so grateful for his efforts that they have named a street after him. He is held in such esteem that his eightieth birthday party had to take place in Wrigley Field to accommodate the crowd.

Central to Father Mac's belief is the understanding that in order to be of service to others we have to begin where they are. We must stop judging them, stop criticizing, comparing, and complaining, and thus become free to be compassionate.

Compassion means to suffer with. It can never coexist with criticism and complaint because these judgments imply superiority and create distance. Compassion is lost in the distance between "us" and "them."

Compassion requires that we leave our illusions of preciousness and security to voluntarily enter a place where we are weak and vulnerable. We must be willing to sacrifice the comfort distance provides. We must fight our instinct to avoid suffering when we cannot find a quick cure for it.

For in denying the needs of others, we diminish ourselves. Compassion is found in the knowledge we all have pain. We are all human. We will all suffer. The adolescent suffers the pain of insecurity and rejection. The wealthy wonder if they are loved for, or in spite of, their money. The elderly feel forgotten and abandoned. Minorities feel discriminated against, left out, and disadvantaged. We all have the need to exercise our compassion and to find support in the compassion of others.

"I think God asks his friends to do the hard things," Father

Mac concludes. "He always puts us on an obstacle course. We have to identify with him. His life was a life of challenge. It was filled with a lot of disasters and a lot of reverses, and the disciple is no greater than the master. When he is asking us to do something hard, it's a testimonial that he loves us and he likes us. God writes the greatest scripts of all."

QUESTIONS:
Who in your life do you find yourself criticizing most often? What can you do to let go of your judgments and close that distance?

GOD'S HAND

"The true meaning of love of one's neighbor is not that it is a command from God which we are to fulfill, but that through it and in it we meet God."

...Martin Burber

"The heart never heals," Mary Jo says. "Bruises heal, but the heart never heals."

An abused child, Mary Jo Copeland struggled most of her life with her self-esteem and feelings of inadequacy. Now she says she would not be who she is without the horrible pain of shivering in her room, going without baths, being kicked down, and ridiculed by kids at school.

Later, as she was beginning to raise her family, her neighbors ignored her or told her husband her behavior was so bizarre she was nuts. "That pain was part of the plan," Mary Jo says, "without it, I wouldn't be sitting here. And I thank God for it."

"Here" is Caring and Sharing Hands, which she started to help the poor in Minneapolis. Each day her organization provides one thousand people with meals, shelter, transportation, and medical care. Over the last fifteen years, she has touched thousands of lives and many lives have touched her. But the one who made the most profound impact was an angry young man named Brian.

Brian lived in a boxcar. One day while he was visiting the shelter, Mary Jo knelt to wash his feet. As she performed this symbolic act of service and love, she felt the anger flow out of him. He told her his story – how he had been beaten by a brother and hurt badly, which lead to his decision to run away at the age of twelve.

"He had bought a knife, put rocks in his pockets for protection and bummed across the country. He had been arrested in all forty-eight contiguous states before he wound up in that boxcar in Minneapolis." Mary Jo said. "People said he was nuts. All I saw was a hurting human being saying, 'Help me.'"

Mary Jo found Brian a bed at the shelter. She brought him pillows and a blanket and let him sleep there for four months. Each morning she would come up and feed him. She spent several thousand dollars on his teeth, got him a driver's license, cleaned him up, and cared for him for more than two years.

"It was not an easy task," she says. "He was angry and violent at times. But there were times when I held his hand and thought – 'This is God's hand.' For all the fighting and screaming and carrying on, there was a piece of Brian that was God's piece. He didn't want to be who he was.

"I knew the amount of anger and fear that lives within this human being was enormous and that he might be threatening to a lot of people. But I also knew that whoever comes into my path, whoever comes in here, we are charged to reach out to, because in Brian, I see myself. Brian is a mirror for Mary Jo Copeland, beating his body, saying 'I can't make it. I'm no good.'

"That's the burden and the joy of helping Brian – the joy of knowing God has given me what it takes to help him. We have to reach out to those who can't quite make it. We are responsible for those people. We are responsible for the little ones who didn't ask to be born. We have to share what we have.

"My goal is to always look to help and not for the outcome. Every soul in this life is worth saving. And every soul can be saved. We don't have to reach thousands if we reach out to one hurting person each day we live."

We can all make the world better because we are in it, Mary Jo reminds us. All you have to do is share. Share your smile. Share your love. We make a difference in this world with our kindness.

"In the evening of life," as Mary Jo says, "we will be judged on only one thing – love. Love until it hurts."

QUESTION:

Does your past give you a kinship with certain people who need your help?

CARING AND SHARING

"The world is pushed forward by men who care; but it is lifted to companionship with the heart of God by men who share."

...*Henry Sloan Coffin*

John Van Hengel founded the first food banks in this country more than a quarter of a century ago. In 1976 he set up Second Harvest, which counsels other people interested in setting up food banks and supports the more than two hundred food banks in the United States and around the world.

Van Hengel did not come easily to his task. In his twenties, he had a penchant for the good life. He played tennis with movie stars and volleyball on Muscle Beach. He married a model, worked as a theatrical agent, studied broadcasting, ran a restaurant, and drove a beer truck.

John said he found the key to a new life in the Scriptures. He found Matthew 6 particularly meaningful: "Lay not upon yourselves treasure upon earth where moth and rust doth corrupt and where thieves break through and steal. But lay up for yourselves treasures in heaven for where your treasure is, there will your heart be also."

With this inspiration, John gave everything away, putting himself firmly out on faith. He worked for ten years without a salary. He found his clothes at the Salvation Army and lived in a room above a garage. He wanted to "own" as little as possible.

Twenty years later, John still relies on the benevolence of

others as much as they rely on him. "The clothes that I wear are all given to me," he says. "Everything I have has been given to me and it's better this way. This way, someone else can give and I can receive. Then I can give. The whole thing is a rapport of giving and sharing."

The joy of living in society in Van Hengel's understanding is that each person can derive benefits from other people's efforts. Each person contributes a little and then receives a vast benefit of society's achievements.

"I just enjoy giving," Van Hengel says. "Over the years I have learned that the great pleasure in life is to be able to give something. Material things as such don't mean much, but the fact that I have opportunity to share is really fun.

"The Lord didn't put us on this earth to be selfish and to look out only for ourselves. He wanted us to learn to relate to each other. God has given us two hands – one to receive with and the other to give with. We are not cisterns made for hoarding. We are channels made for sharing. But if our hands are fully occupied in holding on to something, we can neither give nor receive."

The only things of real value in life are the things you cannot replace. These are things you can never own, but must share. The things that matter most are the things you can share and not diminish by sharing.

QUESTIONS:

Are you a "cistern" hoarding all you have that is valuable or are you a channel? How much of what you have been given, how much of what you have learned and earned, are you sharing?

S ELFISHNESS

"It is one of the most beautiful compensations of nature that no one can help another without helping himself."

...Ralph Waldo Emerson

One day as we were walking through Give Kids The World Village in Orlando, Henri Landwirth, founder of this resort for terminally ill children, stopped me and said, "You and I are the most selfish people I know."

I remember being surprised and a little embarrassed by his remarks. I know I am not the best person in the world, but I didn't think I was *that* bad.

Knowing he had my attention, Henri continued, "I know in my attempt to give back what this life has given to me, I have personally been given so much more than I have ever imagined. Much more. Most people have no idea how much we get out of what we are doing."

In the years since that time, I have often wondered – who has the greater need? The one who is helped or the one who helps? Sometimes it seems the most selfless thing we can do is also the most selfish. Everything we give produces great dividends that we can then reinvest.

Dave Thomas, founder of Wendy's International, agrees. "A lot of the time when you are taking care of someone else you are really helping yourself," he said. "It seems to me like the more you can help someone else and put yourself second the better it works out for you."

The reward for the giver is always greater than the gift.

QUESTIONS:

How would Henri Landwirth describe you? Are you selfish or self-centered?

III

FORGET YOURSELF

"Whatever there is of God and goodness in the universe, it must work itself out and express itself through us. We cannot stand aside and let God do it."

...Albert Einstein

The Reason
We Are Here

The earliest human records reflect man's search for meaning and purpose. Through the generations, from culture to culture, from religion to religion, from Moses to Mohammed, Christ to Buddha, one answer is constant: We are here to love each other.

The Torah reminds us, "Deeds of love are worth as much as all the commandments of the law." Christians are bound to "love one another as I have loved you." Followers of Islam are taught that "whatever good you do for others, you send before your own soul and shall find with God, who sees all you do." The religions of the East – Hinduism and Buddhism – express the same thought with their admonition to "hurt none by word or deed, be consistent in your well-doing."

From this fundamental truth, reflected in these differing ways of saying the same thing, flows man's mission statement. Everything man does that matters is done in response to this central law of life. Everything that lasts was created as the result of love and concern for others.

We are most fully human *and* most like God when we are creating and when we are caring. Creating has to do with what you bring *into* the world, caring with what you do *for* the world. The desire to do one inspires the other.

The solution to all the problems we face, the answer to the most complicated questions we will ever encounter can be found in the love and concern of one human being for another.

The Design of the Universe

"I have learned silence from the talkative, tolerance
from the intolerant, and kindness from the unkind."

...*Gibran*

In Henri Landwirth I see the design of the universe. He has suffered more adversity and experienced more joy than most of us can imagine.

Henri is one of the youngest survivors of the Holocaust. Separated from his family while still a boy, he survived five different camps before finding freedom.

In all, Henri spent five years in the closest thing to hell that humans can contrive. Separated from his twin sister Margot and any vestige of civilization, Henri lived in a world without kindness, yet the love of life this unkindness kindled inspires all who come to know him.

"The first thing that happened was my father was taken by the Germans to a prison in the ghetto," Henri remembers. "After the war, I found out he was shot. My mother lasted almost the whole war. Two weeks before the end of the war, they took my mother and about two thousand other prisoners on board a boat and exploded it in the Stuttgart harbor."

Henri, too, was marked for death several times, narrowly escaping each time. His last escape from death led to liberation. As the Allies approached the camp where Henri was kept, the guards marched Henri and a couple of dozen others out into the woods. When Henri protested, a guard struck him on the back of the head and left him for dead in the ditch.

Later when he returned to consciousness, he found everyone else was gone. As he wandered around in a daze, he found the others lying in the woods where they had been shot. He fled in fear, hiding for days and scrounging for food until, to his surprise, he found himself surrounded by Americans, not Germans.

After the war, with the help of relatives who loaned him passage, Henri made his way to the United States. Within three months of his arrival, he received another surprise – he was drafted to fight in Korea.

"I really thought that somebody was playing a joke on me," Henri says. "Who is this sending me a telegram from the president giving me greetings? I didn't speak any English and couldn't even read the telegram. I thought someone was trying to be funny."

But looking back, Henri will tell you this was "one of the best things that anybody could have done for me," proving the adage that "troubles are just tools by which God fashions us for finer things."

Henri went into the Army an immigrant with limited skills and no knowledge of the English language. He came out an American with the opportunity to go to school under the GI Bill.

Henri applied himself and learned hotel management. He worked as a bellhop, a desk clerk, and a night manager before being offered the chance to manage a hotel in a little place called Cape Canaveral. The Starlight Motel, as it was known, was the first hotel at the cape. It was soon to become famous as the "home away from home" for the *Mercury 7* astronauts.

"I got caught up in the world of business and making money and making more money and building more and making more," Henri says. "And I really, honestly had not found the fulfillment that I was looking for."

Then came the moment when Henri's past and present came together. Unexpectedly, he received a call from a foundation looking for a place to house a sick little girl whose wish was to see DisneyWorld. Henri rapidly agreed, but the child died before the foundation could put the other pieces of the wish together. When Henri heard the news, he swore this would never happen again.

From Henri's promise has come a miracle called Give Kids the World. Over thirty thousand terminally ill children from around the world have visited this joyful village in the eleven years since it was created.

Henri reminds me there is no way to make sense of the world from a personal point of view. There is no personal answer to the question, "Why me?" Why are some so blessed? Why are others so troubled? How do you explain any of the events that mark our lives in terms of merit and worth, behavior and belief?

The only way the world makes sense is from a distance. With a larger view we can see how the pieces fit together, how what happens to one is often for the benefit of another, and how completely we need each other to be whole.

Part of the evidence of this is the fact that no one is fully happy until he finds the purpose for which God intended him. For Henri, it came with the completion of the circle. He was already a successful man and a millionaire many times over when he answered that little girl's call. But he will tell you, in spite of all that, his life was curiously empty. In the village he created for the children, he found the piece of himself he lost in the Nazi concentration camps.

"Since we started Give Kids the World," he says, "I feel like somebody came along and gave me a gift – a gift of life – and that's all I want to do." Henri says. "I have a deep understanding of what's going on with these children and their parents. Because I have seen death."

From the nearness of death has come life; from hate has come miraculous love. "For a long time I never thought that miracles existed," Henri said. "As I became involved with Give Kids the World, I am convinced that they exist in our lives. I see them almost daily."

QUESTION:
What have you experienced, suffered, and learned that might be of benefit to others?

STEPPING OUT ON FAITH

"Faith is the first factor in a life devoted to service. Without faith, nothing is possible. With it, nothing is impossible."

...*Mary McCloud Bethune*

"I am a kid like these kids," Donnalee Velvick said.

She spoke from a swing in the backyard of a firehouse she

turned into a home for her sixty kids some twenty years ago.

"I made a promise when I was eleven that if I could ever get out of the mess I was in I would spend my life helping other kids," Donnalee said. "I didn't want anyone else to go through what I was going through."

Few people have been through as much.

Donnalee was born in a maternity home in Los Angeles. She never met her father. Her mother, who was thirteen, put her up for adoption. Instead of getting a home and a loving family, she was placed with the principals of a child pornography ring. She lived with fear and degradation until the age of twelve when she ran away.

Donna then lived in hiding for two more years while the police searched for the survivors of the ring. All her childhood memories are of "work and hiding, moving from place to place and discipline to keep my mouth shut." There was no television or radio. She was not allowed to talk with the neighbors and can't recall a friend until she got to high school.

Over the last twenty-two years, Donnalee has made a home for more than three hundred children who have been similarly tormented and traumatized. The summer I visited, there were thirty-six children with her under the age of eighteen, nine over the age of eighteen, eleven disabled children, and eighteen dogs.

Like Donnalee, most of these children carry the scars of the past. Many of the girls have words like "Daddy, No" cut into their stomachs with Bic pens, scissors, or other sharp instruments. Others, including most of the boys – who have also been raped – have just sliced themselves up because they wanted to die. All of them carry mental baggage, suffer post-traumatic stress disorder, and are educationally slow.

"We have a few loving parents who weren't the ones who abused the child – it was a day care worker or a school teacher and their kids are just not able to function," Donnalee says. "But they're angry at mom and dad because mom and dad didn't provide a safe environment. So inside our property lines is that 'safe place.' But the most important thing is that this is home."

Donnalee bought the converted firehouse she calls home in 1976. At the time, the doors were falling off and the windows were broken out. There were holes in the roof and pigeons had roosted inside.

"It was simply terrible," she remembers, "but it was big and the owner was willing to accept nine thousand down and take a chance on someone who had no job, no prospects, and a lot of kids to take care of."

Donnalee sold scraps of fabric on the street corner to make the mortgage. The first winter her family went without utilities and slept in the basement. The front yard still carries the reminder of that cold winter in the form of seven stumps from trees cut down for heat.

Then came more kids and a little fabric store and then a secondhand shop in town whimsically named "Hopefully Yours." That store clears the princely sum of twenty-five thousand dollars a year. Another six thousand a year comes in from a gift-wrapping booth at the mall during the holidays and a couple of local fund-raisers organized by community groups.

It isn't a lot, but somehow Donnalee and her family get by.

"I open an envelope in the morning and I don't know what's in it," Donnalee says. "We get maybe five envelopes a day. There can be three one-dollar bills or there could be a check for one hundred dollars. After we pay the basic house payments and utilities, we make a decision on what food we'll have."

Donnalee calls it "stepping out on faith."

"I start each day with just one simple reminder," she explains. "Matthew, sixth chapter, twenty-fifth through thirty-first verse. It says seek the Lord and don't worry about what you are going to eat or what you are going to wear. I believe in that.

"I don't know what's going to come to that door, but I know I'm going to work the hardest I know how. If there's a sack of potatoes or if it's some carrots or celery – whatever comes – we can use it and add to our pantry."

The hardest part of all this for Donnalee and the only thing she worries about is having to say, as she often does, that there is no more room at the inn. Her consolation is the knowledge that many of her kids have gone out as adults to do what she has done, and are helping others.

"My kids are here in town, on the mission fields, and all over the country helping other people," she says with satisfaction.

When I asked her the greatest lesson she has learned, she responded. "Life has taught me that no matter how big the bump in the road, there is an option. You can sit there, complain about the bump, and not move. Or you can go over it, under it, or around it. You have the choice."

For Donnalee, the choice is always clear. "I know that this is what I need to be doing. All I want to do is serve until the day comes that God calls me home."

QUESTIONS:

Donnalee Velvick steps out on faith. Daily she depends on providence to provide. Is your faith that strong? What is your heart telling you to do, telling you to trust, and your fear forbidding you to try?

WALKING ON WATER

"I thank God for my handicaps, for through them, I have found myself, my work, and my God."

...Helen Keller

Unlike Henri Landwirth and Donnalee Velvick, Evelyn duPont's early years were golden. Raised in an upper-middle-class family, she was a swimming champion in Canada and the United States. She was good enough to compete in the Olympics before settling down to raise a family in California.

Then, when she was forty, Evelyn was stricken with polio. "It was really a terrible thing," she said. "I had been so active all my life, then 'boom' – I couldn't walk or get around by myself. But no matter what they said, I felt I had to get on with my life."

The doctors steeled her commitment by telling her that she would never walk again, let alone swim. "That was the last straw," Evelyn told me. "A doctor isn't God. I said to myself, 'I may not be able to walk on water but I can certainly swim in it.'"

With determination, discipline, and the will of her champion's heart, Evelyn built a swimming pool and initiated her own hydrotherapy program. It was nothing fancy, she remembers; she just submerged herself in warm water every day and worked at it.

Evelyn worked at it all day, every day, seven and eight hours at a time. It took years, but finally she began to be able to walk. Evelyn supported herself by walking in between twin beds until she could stand upright without fear of falling.

Ten years after she began, Evelyn had the satisfaction of having proven the doctors wrong. She had also learned something important about herself in the process. "I knew I'd be responsible for teaching anybody I came in touch with how to get in and out of water with a measure of confidence."

Her teaching process began as she walked through the neighborhood on her crutches. "I'd see a little child with a disability and we'd get to talking and I'd say, 'If you want to swim why don't you come over to my backyard,'" Evelyn said. "Soon the word got around and it was just like Lourdes of Long Beach."

Within two years, kids from everywhere had heard of Evelyn duPont and were making their pilgrimage to her healing waters. They came in gurneys, wheelchairs, braces, and crutches until the demand for her pool became so great she had to run it in shifts.

When her pool was no longer big enough, she began raising money and built a community pool. Since that time, more than a quarter of a million disabled people have come to Evelyn looking for help. California Pools for the Handicapped, as her program became known, works with them to instill confidence and self-worth.

"My philosophy is basically to teach people they are worthy of going on, they are worthy of sharing the experience of life," Evelyn told me. "A person, when they become disabled or are born disabled, is always told what they can't do. They are told they can't walk, can't see, or can't hear. When they come into the pool, we teach them what they *can* do.

"I think they can do absolutely anything if they really have the desire and try. I *know* anyone who has the desire can learn to swim. It may take two or three years, but they can learn. Quadriplegics included," Evelyn said. "I had one man in here with cerebral palsy so bad it took two life jackets just to keep him afloat. But he wanted to learn to swim and he did."

Carol Bolles's daughter is a perfect example of Evelyn's success. Born without arms and legs, her disability predicted a bleak future. As a last resort, Mrs. Bolles brought her daughter to California Pools for the Handicapped, and Evelyn began teaching her about the outside world.

When she learned Evelyn had passed away, Mrs. Bolles wrote the following tribute: "I was very skeptical of what Evelyn told me at first. After all, my daughter was less than a year old. But soon, I was seeing her floating and swimming. Her eyes would open wide as she smiled and floated in the warm water.

"A year later, Mrs. duPont presented my daughter with an award for her achievement. It was a bronze medallion that bore the insignia of *Apollo XIV*, complete with the American flag and a replica of the astronauts. We have always kept it as a reminder of my daughter's first success.

"Sunday after Evelyn died, I came upon the award and put it on the kitchen counter so I could mail it to my daughter.

She now works at Kennedy Space Center as a safety engineer. I will mail it to her, along with the obituary.

"Evelyn gave us hope. She opened the door for my daughter's success and independence."

QUESTION:

Hope is the other side of fear. All it takes to pass through is a willing heart. Look at your handicaps, your feared and broken places. What is the well below the emptiness?

THE PURPOSE OF LIFE

"It is good for us to think that no grace or blessing is truly ours till we are aware that God has blessed someone else with it through us."

...Phillip Brooks

Truett Cathy's first business was selling Coca-Cola door to door at the age of eight. He is enough of a businessman to still remember that he made a nickel for profit on each half-dozen Cokes he sold. Later, he began buying Cokes by the case – twenty-four for eighty cents – and thought "that was big business."

Today Truett runs Chick-fil-A, a company he started with his brother right after World War II. The two brothers pooled their resources to open a small restaurant called the Dwarf House.

"We had four thousand dollars between us and borrowed six thousand more. We were determined to be successful," Truett says, "because we couldn't afford to fail. Everything was at stake."

The restaurant was open twenty-four hours a day, six days a week. As a measure of his commitment, Truett took a room next door so that he could be there at any hour. From that humble beginning, Chick-fil-A, now a four-hundred-million-dollar company, was born.

It is a remarkable story, by any account. But what makes it most remarkable is the way Truett Cathy chooses to operate his company.

"Some ten years ago, we asked ourselves: Why are we in business?" Truett says. "Why are we alive? What is the purpose of living anyway? After days of discussion we came up with the following statement of our corporate purpose: to be faithful stewards of all that is entrusted to our care and to have a positive influence on all the people with whom we come in contact.

"Whether we know it or not, we influence everyone we associate with in a positive or negative way," Truett explains. "The ability to influence another person by what we do is probably one of the greatest gifts God has given us."

Truett's fidelity to this objective is evident in the way he treats his franchise holders, his employees, and the public. For example, while most franchises charge heavy entrance fees, often hundreds of thousands of dollars, Chick-fil-A charges none and guarantees new franchise holders a minimum wage until their franchise is established.

In addition, despite the competition and the loss of revenue, Truett closes every one of his franchises – many of them located in shopping malls – every Sunday so that his employees can keep the Sabbath.

The company sponsors a scholarship program that guarantees educational assistance to every employee. "There are no strings attached to the scholarship," Truett says, "other than that they stay on the job at least two years."

So far the company's educational commitment to its employees exceeds $8 million. While there is no obligation to stay with Chick-fil-A, a third of the franchises are operated by young people who were the recipients of these scholarships.

"I consider myself a bit selfish," Truett says. "I'm really looking out for my own interests. Because I find that when I lose myself and try to invest resources in other people, there is a joy deep down. There is a real reward that comes with the feeling you are contributing to humanity. I think that is the reason we were created.

"You cannot be a success in life unless you develop a heart for other people," Truett concludes. "I say to my wife oftentimes, we are not in the chicken business, we are in the people business. It is each and every one of our responsibilities to use what resources we have to help other people."

Near the end of his life, Einstein was being interviewed for some abstruse scientific publication. As they were wrapping up this convoluted interview, he was asked, "Why are we here?" When he looked puzzled, the interviewer immediately became embarrassed and apologized for asking something so difficult.

Einstein smiled gently and said, "If I looked puzzled it is because you asked me something so simple. We are here to serve one another." It is the service we provide to others that gives meaning and purpose to our lives.

QUESTIONS:

If you are in business, take Truett Cathy's test and ask yourself, "Why?" How does your professional mission statement or the mission statement of your company match your personal mission statement? Is your professional life structured in a way that is consistent with your personal beliefs?

THE GREATEST GIFT

"What you are is God's gift to you and what you do with what you are is your gift to God."

...George Foster

Jon Huntsman recently gave $100 million to fight cancer — the largest single donation ever recorded to that cause. Huntsman, chairman and CEO of the Huntsman Corporation, the nation's largest privately held chemical company, is obviously a generous man. And just in case you're thinking, "Well, he's got plenty to spare," let me tell you that that was far from an isolated action.

Huntsman was contributing a significant amount to the less fortunate when he didn't have a significant amount in the eyes of the world. Even when he began his career in the navy, Huntsman routinely gave $50 of his $250 paycheck to help people in need.

From his Salt Lake City corporate offices, Huntsman oversees operations in eighty-one sites in twenty-three different countries, but he was born into a home so humble it lacked indoor plumbing. His schoolteacher father didn't have much money, but he gave Jon something much more important – a profound sense of right and wrong and the knowledge that he had a responsibility to help others.

Now, Huntsman has all that the world calls success. He is listed in *Forbes* among the wealthiest Americans, has been an advisor to presidents, and is universally admired as a self-made man. For him, all is simply an opportunity to be of greater service.

In 1988, for example, when a devastating earthquake wiped out one-sixth of the Armenian population, Huntsman saw the need and the opportunity almost immediately. He began by sending millions of dollars for food and medical supplies. Then, realizing that nearly half a million people had been left homeless after the quake, Huntsman established a plant in Armenia to make precast concrete. In so doing, he provided the material necessary for new homes while simultaneously creating jobs for Armenians at a time when their economy was faltering.

Huntsman has given millions of dollars to each of Utah's three major universities and is a generous supporter of the Bennion Center, the Aston Scholarship Fund, the Jake Garn

Institute, and various medical research programs at the University of Utah. He is a devout Mormon and has given much time and money to his church, but he is also a significant contributor to work of other churches. At one time, he was listed as the largest single contributor to Catholic Charities in the country.

To hear his friends tell it, this is just part of his nature. J. W. Marriott, chairman and president of Marriott International, Inc., has known Huntsman for over twenty-five years and says, "Jon is the most giving person I have ever met. Some people like golfing, some like to drive fast cars. Well, Jon likes giving his money away. He loves life and he loves people and this is his way of expressing his genuine compassion for others."

"Money has never been our objective or goal in our family," Huntsman explains. "Therefore, sharing it has never been difficult. The amassing of wealth is one of the worst species of idolatry. No idol is more debasing.

"If somebody came and said, 'We could find a cure for cancer if you'd give not $100 million, but everything you have,' I'd say, 'Great. Take it. I'll start over again.' I wouldn't even think two minutes about it. I'd go home, take my wife out to McDonalds instead of the New York Broiler, and it wouldn't bother me."

He isn't kidding about giving it all away. That is his specific intent. "For the last ten years, as everyone in this office knows, my only focus in continuing to build this business is that all of it goes," he says. "I mean, all of it goes eventually to our foundation, which in turn will give it out to people in need throughout the world."

B. C. Forbes observed, "It's so much easier to do good than

to be good." Jon Huntsman does both. His life has balance and focus. Although his keen business sense has afforded him a life of luxury, Huntsman's modest but loving upbringing and his deep faith in God have guided him to use his wealth, his time, and his talents well. He is more interested in benefiting millions than making millions. In fact, he considers the acquisition of wealth "simply a by-product of fulfilling work."

For all that he has, all that he has been given, Jon Huntsman has found his greatest satisfaction in simply loving his fellow man. His is the gift of a lifetime.

QUESTIONS:

Jon Huntsman's gift is a lifetime of caring. How would a stranger evaluate your life?

Thomas Jefferson, arguably the ablest American who ever lived, picked the words he wanted on his tombstone. He asked to be remembered only as the author of the Declaration of Independence and the Virginia Statute on Religious Freedom and as the founder of the University of Virginia. If there is one thing you would like to be remembered for, if there was to be something carved in granite to rest over your head for eternity, what would you want it to be?

CHERISH THE CHILDREN

A child is God's opinion that the world should go on. In cherishing the children, we care for the seeds of ourselves and hope of our future. We all know this to be true intuitively, yet, as Grandma Edie and Vantrease Russell can testify, the biggest problem in America today is the unloved child.

Last year a mixed breed mutt made national news when she repeatedly faced fire to rescue her litter of pups from danger. Not long after that, three infants turned up abandoned and dead in Orange County, California. One was found in the surf, another on the beach, and the third was discarded in a cardboard box. These were not isolated events. On average, twenty newborn infants are killed in this country every month.

Less drastic, but equally sobering are the statistics reported recently that indicate that the average adult male spends less than thirty seconds a day in meaningful contact with his preschool children. At the same time, there is evidence that the same child will be placed before the electronic baby-sitter we call a television for at least four hours a day. Small wonder then that the values of our children are often so much at odds with the values we were taught.

We would do well to remember that values are not hereditary. In the words of George S. Benson, "Great ideals and principles do not live from generation to generation just because they are right, nor even because they have been carefully legislated. Ideals and principles continue from generation to generation only when they are built into the hearts of the children as they grow up."

Reverse Education

"True goodness springs from man's own heart. All men are born good."

...*Confucius*

Six months after our first national recognition ceremony for young adults, I got some of the most surprising news I've heard since we founded the Heart of America all those years ago. At the ceremony, we had honored ten young people because they were outstanding in every way. They were model children who had demonstrated leadership and maturity beyond their years, picked from thousands of nominations provided by junior and senior high school principals.

I couldn't help wondering what had made these kids so outstanding? What common denominators could we find? What could we learn from them that might help us multiply their number?

The opportunity to find that out came through the generosity of Senator John Glenn and his colleagues at the *Mercury 7* Foundation. With their help we were able to arrange a week at Space Camp for these kids.

Each night following their Space Camp activities, the kids "came over the wall" to have pizza in my hotel room and talk about their lives. One of those evenings, I asked what they had gotten out of the national recognition they received.

I expected the kids to talk about the scholarships they were given and the relationships they had formed. About the last thing I expected was the response from Cuong. This young man said the best thing to come out of the process for him was that he was finally able to explain to his parents the value of what he was doing.

Frankly, I was floored. These were the golden ones, every parent's delight. I had naively assumed that they were what they were because of the values instilled at home, that they did what they did not only with parental support, but with their parents' enthusiastic encouragement.

To the contrary, as I went around the room I found half of the ten kids were doing what we had honored them for doing without parental support. Several were acting in the face of outright opposition at home.

In the years since, I have made it a point to ask each of our young adult recipients about parental support. While many do have idyllic backgrounds and fully supportive families, I consistently discover that about half of them don't.

"There are obviously two educations," James T. Adams wrote. "One should teach us how to make a living. The other should teach us how to live." I have come to the conclusion that we may be succeeding at one, but we are certainly failing at the other.

Real education should bring us out of self into something far finer – into an understanding that links us with all humanity. Increasingly, I wonder if we are not engaged in the opposite, a perverse practice that teaches kids to forget and ignore their best instincts.

About a year ago, I mentioned my experience with the kids at Space Camp to Pam and Henri Landwirth, the founders of the Give Kids the World Village in Orlando. Pam became quiet, then said, "I just realized I'm doing the same thing."

I was surprised again. Pam has two of the best and brightest girls I have ever seen.

"The kids are always asking to go down to the Village," she said. "and I'm always saying they can, but only after they do their chores or their homework. It's always conditional. They always have to do something else first. What I just realized is that the message I am sending them is that these other things are more important. Whatever I want them to do at the moment, however mundane, is more important than what they want to do – help sick kids."

It may be that this "reverse education" accounts for much of the meanness of our times. If so, we should realize we educate the goodness out of our kids at our own peril. It is this spirit – the spirit of caring and concern for our neighbor – that distinguishes us from the beasts. It is the identity that comes from loving others as ourselves that creates community. Without that sense of community, civilization would not exist and man would be reduced to being what many say he once was, just another animal, larger, smarter, and meaner than most, set loose to ravage the world.

QUESTIONS:

Are you showing your children what they can do to help take care of others, or are you only teaching them how to take care of themselves? Are you more concerned that they know how to make a living or how to live?

T H E R E   A R E   N O   B A D   K I D S

"The only thing we can never get enough of is love.
And the only thing we can never give enough of is
love."

...Henry Miller

Grandma Edie Lewis remembered her father as a difficult man
and not a particularly good role model.

"He was a bootlegger," she says, "then he went into moon-
shine. All of his friends were moonshiners and hijackers, and
he wasn't the easiest person to get along with. Every time you
looked at him cross-eyed, he'd pull his belt out."

As a result, Edie left home when she was sixteen and went
to work to support herself. She was in her seventies when I
spoke with her, but the memory of what it was like to be a dis-
placed kid had always stayed with her.

These days Grandma Edie lives in Texas, and for the last
thirty years, she has cared for kids discarded by our society.
These are the street kids, addicts, alcoholics, and gang members that most people believe to be beyond redemption. She
believes that there are no bad kids, just a lot of bad parents.

"I didn't start out doing this on purpose," Lewis said. "It
just evolved after I found a kid sleeping in my backyard."

Grandma Edie was living in Alaska at the time. She heard a
dog barking at about two in the morning. When she went out
to investigate, she found a teenage boy sleeping against her
house, trying to keep warm.

"He was only seventeen, but big, like a football player," she recalls. When she asked him where he lived and why he wasn't sleeping at home, she was surprised to hear him say, "My family doesn't want me.

"I was so naive to bad parents then," Grandma Edie says. "I thought every parent loved their kid. I just *knew* they were worried sick with the thought he might be lying dead or hurt somewhere."

When she called his parents to let them know he was safe, his father responded – "You found him, you keep him" – and slammed the phone down. The next day she called again and the boy's father was even more irate. "I told you we didn't want him!" he said. "You can have him."

Edie found out that the boy's parents had made him quit school at fifteen to go to work to support their drinking and drug habits. They beat him and verbally abused him until he had enough and ran away.

Edie took him in. Over the next few months the word got around. One kid after another began knocking on her door. "I kept saying what's one more?" she recalls. "First thing you know, I had a full-fledged shelter going."

When she moved to Texas eighteen years ago, her work followed her. Since then Grandma Edie has taken in over three hundred kids. She says the common denominator is that none of them has had a decent role model or lived in a good home.

"The child abuse stories are almost unbelievable," she says. "With the abuse and parents that don't care, parents on drugs and messing around with different partners, daughters getting raped by their mother's boyfriends and father's pimping for their sons, it becomes unbearable. It is no wonder they leave home."

"They wind up in the seedy parts of town where all the pimps and whores are selling themselves or they get hooked on drugs at an early age. They've had a lot of bad teachers and they don't know what else to do."

The kids she cares for are young adults – late teens and early twenties – hardened by the streets, hooked on drugs. Many of them have been drawn into satanic cults or gangs like the Bloods and the Crips.

"The general public feels that once they've reached this age – eighteen, twenty-two, twenty-three, twenty-four – they'll never get it together and it's a waste of time and money to try to reach them," Edie says. "But they don't know the circumstances that brought them to this point. If any one of them had been brought up in a halfway decent home, they probably wouldn't have turned out the way they did. It's not their fault, but they are the ones who get punished for it.

"When they arrive here I'm usually looking at a sad sight," she says. "They're hungry, they're dirty, they're broke, many of them are hooked on drugs, and they're all scared. They've never had an adult in their life they can trust. A lot of them hear about me for quite a while before they knock on my door. When they come, it's because they're desperate and don't know what else to do."

Grandma Edie cares for them with her Social Security and a small annuity from her husband's death. When the money runs out, she takes a bucket or a jug and goes door to door or stands out by the highway.

"I don't like doing that," she says, but she prefers begging to borrowing or getting government funds.

The kids stay as long as they need to – six months, a year,

two years. While they may move on, they never really leave. "I'm always their grandma," she says with pride. "I'm their only family. This is home. It's not an institution. The windows aren't barred and the doors aren't locked. In any other place, the first time the kids cause trouble, they kick them out. The first time they backslide, they are gone. I just pick them up, dust them off, give them a hug and another chance.

"It's hard to stay off that stuff. Unless you've been on it, you don't know. You are going to backslide, but eventually they make it, if they want to. You just can't give up on them."

That's the secret, she says. "You don't quit and you let them know you care. They know I don't get paid. I don't take any money from them and I won't take any money from the government. After a few months they realize the only reason I do this is because I really do care. Then they start caring back and I've got them.

"I guess I'm addicted too," she concludes, "very heavily addicted. I can get them off their addictions, but I can't get off mine. My addiction is them. I'm addicted to these kids."

QUESTIONS:

Grandma Edie is addicted to her kids. What's your addiction? What is there that you can't get enough of?

L O V E ' S   W A Y

"We do not believe in ourselves until someone reveals
that deep inside us something is valuable, worth listening to, worthy of our trust, sacred to our touch.
Once we believe in ourselves we can risk curiosity,
wonder, spontaneous delight or any experience that
reveals the human spirit."

...e.e. cummings

"Anybody who doesn't think God has a sense of humor should
look at me," Bill Milliken says. "I was a high school dropout.
The last thing anyone thought I would be doing is something
in education."

What Milliken is doing is running the largest dropout
prevention program in the country – Communities in
Schools. Communities in Schools has touched the lives of
over one hundred thousand children with programs in over
six hundred schools.

Milliken was born to an alcoholic mother. His father
worked hard and was often away from home. From an early
age, Bill was on his own. He ran away many times when he
was a boy and then, the day after he turned sixteen, he took
off for good.

Fortunately, he didn't get far. Milliken ran into a group of
people who worked with troubled kids in the neighborhood. It took them about a year, but finally they began to
turn him around.

"That's when I learned that love goes where people are," he says. "They came in our face and loved us into change. I don't know any other way to explain it. It was the first time somebody believed in me."

From that experience came Milliken's commitment to go back onto the streets, but this time to do something constructive. He and a friend began in Harlem.

If you ask him about those early days, he will tell you what he remembers most is burying eighteen friends. "I'd walk in and see them dead in my bunk from overdoses – people we failed with. So you couldn't very well think in terms of success. You just had to be faithful and not give up."

In New York Milliken initiated the first street academies for young people. He developed programs for children who were being failed by traditional schools. But if you ask him what he has learned along the way, he is quick to say, "Programs don't change people, relationships do.

"What we are seeing are kids dropping out of school and we blame the schools," he explains. "When I went inside the schools, I saw the teachers were just as isolated and lonely as the kids. So I said there's something deeper here. We have had a breakdown in community."

Milliken believes that there are four basic things that kids need: "First and foremost," he says, "they need to have a personal relationship with a caring adult. Second, every child needs a place where they are physically and emotionally safe. Third, every kid needs a chance to give back. And fourth, we have to build a system where every kid has marketable skills. We haven't freed anybody up until they can take care of themselves and their families."

The catalytic factor, the secret ingredient that leavens Milliken's mix, is love. "The secret to turning a kid around is that there has to be at least one adult with an irrational belief in his or her future," he says. "Whoever believed I could make it had to be irrational. There are so many kids out there that nobody believes in. There are so many kids out there that nobody wants.

"I have discovered that the real issues aren't what we call the issues. The issue I've heard over thirty years is, 'Hey, 'I'm lonely, nobody knows my name. I feel worthless, nobody believes in me.' It doesn't take a program. There isn't going to be any education reform, there isn't going to be any change out there unless you start with love. It's love that acts.

"I tell kids, don't believe what they tell you about yourself. Most of the people I have met that are doing anything worthwhile are ordinary people doing extraordinary things. They've been conditioned to believe in IQs and you can do it or you can't do it, and I say all that's a myth. Follow love's way, no matter how tough it is."

QUESTIONS:

Is there someone who has had an irrational belief in your future? Whom have you loved into change?

THE GIFT OF A CHILD

"Help a child and you help humanity."

...*Phillip Brooks*

Vantrease Russell started keeping children as a favor for her friends and neighbors. "I had children at home," she said, "and it was no problem, if they had one or two, to leave them with me if they needed to go to town or something."

Since then, the ones and twos have multiplied by tens and twenties, the moments by months, and the months by years.

One of these children is Marilyn. She was born with a severe handicap. She came to stay with Vantrease fifty-two years ago so that her family could get a little rest. Marilyn is still there.

Then there is the boy who has been with Vantrease for forty-four years, a girl who has been with her for forty years, and another who was born without a backbone and without eyes and has been with Vantrease for thirty-six of her forty years. To date, more than twelve hundred children have gone through her doors. At the moment, the youngest charge she has is a boy who was burned in a fire that left him blind. He is eight now and has been with her since he was three. The smallest person she has is an eighteen-year-old girl who weighs only twenty-four pounds. The largest is a twenty-year-old who weighs over three hundred pounds.

"It was always a challenge to me to take a child that somebody couldn't do nothing with," Vantrease says. "Not too many people pay attention to the handicapped and the retarded. I've had businesspeople say, 'Why do you spend your time with them?' They don't understand that I love them. It's just that simple."

Vantrease grew up with what she calls "the idea of being careful of the handicapped." Her father's sister was an invalid and confined to a wheelchair. A strong woman and an astute businesswoman, this aunt made a strong impression. Still, Vantrease will tell you she didn't have any plan to start an organization.

"It wove around me like a spider web," she said. "It was all word of mouth. I never had a sign out or nothing. Nobody ever knew this was a children's home."

As the word got around, people came to her from miles around with children they couldn't handle, often leaving them anonymously on her doorstop in the middle of the night. Whatever the circumstances, Vantrease's response has always been the same. She has never said 'No' to a child.

"I do for the children," she says, "but there is often another issue around that child. If I can ease that problem, save a marriage, prevent abuse, take the pressure off a relative, I'm happy to do that. It makes me feel good to know that I can do something for somebody."

Vantrease relies on her faith and the community for support. "Everything in this home has been donated," she told me. "Every piece of equipment has come from some individual or organization. People will call me up and say, 'What do you need?' There isn't anyone in this community who hasn't been part of the home some way."

A while back, mindful of her advancing age, a private house was built on the back of the property for Vantrease. She has yet to spend a night there, preferring to sleep near the children.

"It's not that I don't have confidence in my workers," she

says. "It's just my feeling that I'm responsible for these kids and everything going on in this home. I want to be where they are.

"Some people think caring for these children is depressing. It isn't. They don't know our problems. They live in a world of their own. All they know is love. Other people think they may be dangerous, and some are, but all you have to do is understand them and work with them. The angrier a child gets, sometimes, the more love you have to give."

For Vantrease life is nothing but an opportunity to do something for a child. "I need them just as much as they need me," she says. "My life wouldn't be worth two cents without these children. I couldn't live without them."

QUESTION:
Is there something as central to your being as the children are to Vantrease?

IT TAKES A LOT OF HOMES TO MAKE A VILLAGE

"Whenever one life touches another we help or hinder. There is no escape – man drags man down or lifts man up."

...Booker T. Washington

Fifteen years ago, Kent Amos's son came home from school with some new friends. "The boys were okay," Kent said, "but they weren't the kind of kids I thought my son should associate with."

Kent's first thought was to forbid his son to associate with such a rough crowd. He thought they would drag his son down. Then, he had a second thought – why not lift the others up?

"We embraced those children," he told me. "We said if they were going to be *in* this house, they are going to be *of* this house. If they are going to be around this house, this house is going to be their home. If you care for your child, how could you not care for his friends?"

With that, Kent and his wife, Carmen, embarked on an effort to provide African-American teenagers in the District of Columbia with a loving, caring, and disciplined environment. They opened their home and wallet to an extended family that now numbers more than one hundred. They provided an atmosphere free of hopelessness and crime and full of encouragement, guidance and love – a place to call home.

At first, the Amos "family" just met four nights a week and, to hear him describe it, Kent simply did what any good parent would do. He talked with them, checked their report cards, provided support, and encouraged them to do their best.

Now as many as twenty-five kids a night meet in the Amos home. The teenagers enjoy a family dinner and two hours of learning without TV or radio. And their education doesn't stop with their homework. They learn something about life, values, and themselves.

Kent has guided nineteen of his kids through high school and college. Eighteen more are in college at this time. Kent is paying full tuition for four of them and helping the rest. All in all, he has invested more than half a million dollars in his extended family over the years.

Kent firmly believes that the source of most of the difficulties these children face is that they have not been taught the values necessary to withstand temptation and stay out of trouble. "You keep hearing that we may be the first generation that will not give to the next generation more than was given to us. But the people who say that are measuring things, not values. We seem to be more worried about giving children what we didn't have than about giving them what we were given.

"These children themselves have the ultimate decision on almost everything they do," he says, "starting at a very young age. I am trying to get them to internalize a set of values. They need to know there are things of value, but values transcend things."

Kent does what he does because he considers himself fortunate. Although he was blessed with a more privileged upbringing than most of his contemporaries and was surrounded by a positive and supportive family, he remembers flirting with crime and temptations provided by many of his peers. He never excelled academically and it was not until after a seven-year stint in the army that he completed college.

"I learned it is never too late to turn your life around or too early to start," he says.

After college, Kent spent fifteen years with the Xerox Corporation, working his way up through a series of sales and management positions. After his retirement from Xerox, he worked with a consulting group until five years ago when he resigned his position so that he could spend all of his time working with kids.

Kent suggests we live for the infinite. "What is your legacy?" he asks. "No one rises alone. There are always those who contribute to your well-being. Battles were fought for the way of life I enjoy and it is my responsibility to see that way of life continues."

QUESTIONS:

Who contributed to your well-being? What is your legacy?

What would your reaction be if, like Kent Amos, you found your kids associating with some less-than-desirable playmates? Would you be willing to do what he did?

A BEAUTIFUL DREAM

"Our world is saved, one or two people at a time."

...Andre Gide

At the age of fourteen, Eugene Lang was bussing tables in a New York restaurant. "By the strangest fluke," he says, "I was asked to serve the restaurant's best customer, a distinguished man of some reputation."

The gentleman spoke with Lang for a while, then invited him to apply to Swarthmore College, where he had some influence. Lang filled out the required forms dutifully, but he really didn't think he had a chance. To his complete surprise, about three weeks later he received a letter of acceptance and a full scholarship from one of the finest liberal arts colleges in the country.

After he graduated, Lang created a business that licenses

industrial technology around the world. He became deeply involved in education, serving on the boards of Swarthmore and a number of other institutions. Then in 1981, he was invited to give the commencement address to the sixth grade of the public school in East Harlem that he had attended.

"I had nothing prepared to say," Lang recalls, "because the audience was different than any I had come in contact with before." He decided to use Martin Luther King, Jr.'s most famous speech – "I have a dream."

"I told them that they should go on and get educated; that this is the way to realize their dreams, and that they could look forward to going to junior high school, high school and college."

As those words came out of his mouth, Lang said, he realized that these kids had no hope of going to college. He knew there was no way for them to get there.

Suddenly, he found himself saying, "Don't you think for one moment that you can't go to college because right now as a graduation gift, I'm giving each of you a scholarship."

Lang later realized that his dramatic promise to these elementary school children was hollow because most of them would drop out long before they reached college. He felt obligated to do something not only to help them through college but help them get to college as well. "It's a matter of integrity," he says. "When you promise something you make it real."

Out of Lang's determination, the first I Have a Dream program emerged. It began as a personal and private commitment. That changed when Lang learned that every one of his kids had made it to high school, and he realized the power of his promise.

Today there are 156 I Have a Dream projects in fifty-three cities. In each case, one or more sponsors has adopted an entire grade of elementary school children and promised to see them through the high school years with a guaranteed opportunity to go to college.

The key to this program's success is its integrity. "This is not a public relations stunt," Lang says. "We have no angle on this. We truly are interested in this only because we want to see our dreamers thrive.

"When people ask me what it is that I can do as an individual, because the problems are so big, my response is that you must start with the realization that the answer is often very small. The needs of each child represent the totality of all our national problems in microcosm. If you look at it that way then you can find a role worthy of being human. You can find something meaningful to do."

QUESTIONS:

What small answers are in your community? Can you do something to help one child?

Act in Faith

Anything worth doing is an act of faith. Everything we do changes the world though we may never know how. The consequences of our actions are beyond us. They ripple out in ever widening circles until they rebound and return to us amplified, unrecognized, and unrecognizable from places unknown.

In this decade, science and religion, medicine and metaphysics, physics and philosophy have begun to come together. It is as if we have suddenly recognized the truth of the parable of the nine blind men and the elephant – each describing from his perspective the part of the elephant he can sense, while dismissing the perceptions of others.

Finally, we have begun to realize that we are all saying the same thing in the different languages of our disciplines. Take the discovery of the black holes in space. Though they could not be seen or directly measured, scientists concluded that they existed because of the obvious effect they had on the actions of other stellar bodies.

The same phenomenon has been observed in the smallest bits of matter. Everything in the universe is affected by the behavior of everything else. Scientists involved in studies of quantum physics have even discovered that it is no longer possible to consider themselves "objective" or "observers." They have found that they participate in every study and in every experiment with their expectations.

What is true of the stars is true of ourselves. We are influenced by those around us – positively and negatively. In ways largely unseen, we have an impact on each other as our actions and values combine and collide to shape our lives.

In fact, no investment we make in others is as great as our contribution to their belief systems. In the words of Dr. Robert Schuller, "In the power of faith what you believe is what you achieve. Whether we want to or not, all of us live out what we really think and feel deep down inside." What a person thinks and believes, he does and becomes.

The Greatest Sin

"The greatest good you can do for another is not just
to share your riches but to reveal to him his own."

...Benjamin Disraeli

Said to be a classic underachiever, silent, violent, unresponsive, and sullen, a boy named Altheous was destined for a mental institution until a teacher the kids call Momma Hawk rescued him.

"Why are you going to do that to him," Momma Hawk asked the principal. She was told Altheous's homeroom teacher didn't want him near her class because of his temper and poor hygiene.

Under Momma Hawk's "care-full" eye, Altheous blossomed. She found his poor hygiene was the result of living with elderly relatives who did not have a bath, and his temper related to his home life and the abuse that he took from other kids.

Altheous graduated third in his class and won a hockey scholarship to a school in the suburbs. "He's never been a problem," Momma Hawk says with pride. "I'm proud to be part of him. He is phenomenal."

When she came to teach in the inner city of Chicago, Momma Hawk quickly found out writing a problem on the backboard and patting a kid on the back to help them reach the honor roll was not a realistic goal. She found herself in a school with the highest truancy rate in the city. Eighty-one percent of the students dropped out by the ninth grade.

Violence was a daily occurrence and drugs were everywhere.

"I quickly found out you need to do more than say 'no' to drugs," Momma Hawk says. "You can't tell them to say no unless you are taking care of their basic needs."

The more Momma Hawk got involved, the more she found her role transformed. She no longer saw herself as a teacher, but as an ambassador sent to mother the homeless and minister to the neglected, abused, and hopeless children of Chicago.

"I no longer went to work as a teacher," she says of her transformation, "I went to work to love kids. I went to work to hug them and make sure they had food and clothing. I went to work to make sure they felt good about themselves. I knew if I could do that, they would excel."

Momma Hawk's method was simple. She opened her home and her heart to her students. She told them, "If your momma won't feed you, come to my house. If you need a safe place, come stay with me. If you need someone to talk to, I will listen." By treating people as if they were what they ought to be, she helps them become what they are capable of being.

In 1988, Momma Hawk formalized her activities under the name Recovering the Gifted Child. "One might think that it means we are dealing with gifted children just because you hear that terminology," Momma Hawk explains. "But these are children that people have thrown away. I'm recovering the gift within them that I know God gave these kids. My job is to look for something really great in them and develop it and then say, 'Look, that's who you are,' to give them hope and an identity."

In five years, Momma Hawk has only lost two children to teen pregnancy. Sixty-five kids have come through her classroom and become part of her extended family. The school valedictorian in each of the last three years has come out of her class, and the majority of her kids are in the upper 10 percent academically. All of her kids have gone to high school and, in an area where dropping out is the norm, sixty-four of her sixty-five kids are still attending classes.

Momma Hawk's secret is that she understands the greatest sin is the waste of human potential, the waste of a life. Everyone is precious. Everyone is needed. Everybody was born with a purpose. The key to the journey of life is to learn to see ourselves clearly, define our purpose, and fill our potential.

"We cannot perceive whose purpose is what, and why people are, or who they are going to be," Momma Hawk says, "so it behooves us to invest in all of our children. Because the one that is least likely to succeed may be the president and the one that's most likely to succeed may be his secretary.

"We don't realize how our words and actions predict the future of our kids. When we as parents tell them – you're stupid, you're bad, you're dumb, you're never going to amount to anything – they are going to believe us. When I tell these kids – you are gifted, you are my future leaders – they believe me. They could come in here and have no gift at all, but they'll find one just because you told them it is there.

"I can't control the future," she concludes. "I could be working myself to death and still be housing a serial killer. I have no guarantee that I'm not. But I have the assurance that I have given my best and I know most of these children can go out into this society and make a difference. It is said one child, one human being, touches three hundred lives before they leave this world. If you multiply my kids by that number, that's a lot of lives to be touched because of a hug."

QUESTIONS:

Momma Hawk is reclaiming gifts and revealing possibilities. What gifts do you carry that might find a higher expression? What gifts do you see in those near and dear to you that you can nurture?

THE ESSENCE OF LIFE

"A man has made at least a start on discovering the meaning of life when he plants shade trees under which he knows full well he will never sit."

...Elton Trueblood

Most people who know Kevin Johnson know him as the floor leader of the Phoenix Suns, a member of the Dream Team, and a perennial All-Star. We are accustomed to seeing his public face, watching him play ball, and listening to sportscasters interview him about his performance on the court and other issues of the game.

KJ graduated from Sacramento High School in 1983. He led the state in scoring with an average of thirty-two points a game. He became the all-time leader at the University of California in scoring, assists, and steals. As a professional, he has averaged more than twenty points and ten assists a game over the last five seasons.

Few people know what he does when he is not playing ball.

Most people would be surprised to hear him say that he hopes to be remembered more for what he has done off the court than on it.

One of the things KJ has done is found St. Hope Academy in 1989. St. Hope is an extension of home for the children of Sacramento. It provides unconditional love, a safe, comfortable environment, positive role models, training in social skills, and academic tutoring for kids ages eight to seventeen.

Kevin is at St. Hope every day and every night when he's not playing in the NBA. He has dedicated his life to the children there and personally shoulders much of the financial burden of running the place.

He chose the name because hope is his favorite word. "We accomplish nothing without hope," he says. "Hope carries power and strength. The energy behind an activity is equal to the hope in it. If only a few people share such hopes, a power is created nothing can hold down. It inevitably spreads to others."

Hope in this deep and powerful sense is not the same as the vague expectation that things will go well. Rather, it is the ability to work for something because it is good, not just because it stands a chance to succeed. It is what Schweitzer meant when he said, "No ray of sunlight is ever lost, but the green that it wakes needs time to sprout. It is not always granted to the sower to see the harvest."

Not surprisingly, people who work with Kevin at St. Hope describe him as "an earth angel" or "the best role model you have ever met." He does a myriad of "little" things that has made his charity legend in Sacramento.

Talk to people on the street and you will hear how he gave the Mazda RX-7 out of his driveway to a friend in need or sent a check for five thousand dollars to a security guard down on his luck. Kevin donates with such regularity to the elementary school there that it has an annual KJ Day.

"I don't feel that I deserve any credit for any of that," Kevin says. "What I am doing is nothing more than my reasonable responsibility and obligation. In fact, it's easier for someone like me.

"My grandparents were the head of our family and they showed me time and time again how important it is to reach back and pull someone up who may be slipping a little. They didn't have a lot of words, but their example spoke louder than anything. That's what we really need to do when it comes to young people. We can lecture them and come up with all kinds of exercises, but what they are going to remember most is the example we set – what they see.

"What is the essence of life?" he asks. "To serve others, and to do good," he answers. "When people are serving each other, life is no longer meaningless."

QUESTION:
What seeds have you planted that you will never see harvested?

T H E   S E R V I C E   O F   A R T

"We must judge a man's merits not by his great qualities but by the use he makes of them."

...Francois de La Rochefoucauld

When Jacques d'Amboise was a child growing up in Brooklyn,
art was the furthest thing from his mind. When he was forced
to accompany his sister to dance class, he displayed his dis-
pleasure by mugging, mocking, and mimicking the girls at
every opportunity.

The girls' instructor wisely gave him a challenge rather than
a reprimand. "If you are so smart," she said, "let's see if you
can do better." When he responded, she extended the challenge – "Is that as high as you can jump?" Almost before he
knew it and against his will, Jacques was caught up in the
world of dance.

Two years later, at the age of eight, Jacques was sent to study
with Balanchine. He remained the great teacher's favorite
pupil and star performer for forty years.

"Balanchine was wise," Jacques says. "He used music and
dance to express his philosophy, which had almost a religious
bent. He believed man is meant to be in the service of the arts,
the service of mankind, the service of God."

Jacques came to believe that each individual has within him
the possibility of excellence. The purpose of life is to develop
that excellence to the best of his ability. "It's not a competition
with anybody else," he says. "It is a process of inner discovery.
Whatever we do, whatever we can do, we should do our best."

By many accounts, Jacques was the best for more years than most people dance. When he retired, it was widely assumed he would inherit Balanchine's role as director of the New York City Ballet. To everyone's surprise, he decided instead to form his own company – the National Dance Institute. Instead of guiding and refining the movement of some of America's most talented artists, he chose instead to teach poor and underprivileged the children the meaning of art.

"I'm trying to set up environments where I can challenge children to discover the excellence in themselves," Jacques explains. "The performing arts provide a wonderful environment for discovering this quality and enhancing it."

At any given moment, Jacques and his teachers are at work in some thirty different schools in half a dozen states. His teams consists of a composer and conductor, a choreographer, a dance teacher, and a director. Each team focuses on a class of fourth, fifth, or sixth graders and works with them once a week throughout the school year. Over the course of the year, they learn the basics of dance, then how choreography develops, and finally how a performance comes together.

At the end of thirty weeks, all the children are brought together in a theater and shown how the pieces fit together. "In that one day, they meet and rehearse, and one thousand children find out that they are in a two-hour musical and that the steps they learned all fit together with other children. It's extraordinary," Jacques says.

It is a wonderful metaphor for life. For Jacques, all of art seems to be a metaphor for how to live.

"Every performance is your last performance," he says. "It is also your first. You may dance Monday night. But Tuesday you're a different person. And who knows after you dance that night whether you will ever dance again? So each performance becomes the whole world at that moment.

"The only thing we can do is to try and act in the moment. We are making our past. Make it rich and rewarding – not in terms of money – but in terms of that inner discovery of how to make the best of yourself."

QUESTION:
What can you do to establish an environment where you challenge those near you, such as your children, to discover their excellence?

IT STARTS WITH 'WE'

"Many times I realize how much my own outer and inner life is built upon the labors of my fellow men, both living and dead, and how earnestly I must exert myself in order to give in return as much as I have received."

...Albert Einstein

"I cannot do anything," Dave Thomas said. "But we can do anything we want to do. And it takes *we*. I did not build Wendy's. We have built Wendy's. It takes a lot of people."

Dave Thomas is the founder and chairman of Wendy's

International. In twenty-five years Wendy's has grown from one restaurant to over forty-five hundred worldwide. Dave's congenial face is familiar to millions from his television commercials, but he is most proud of his role as the nation's leading advocate of adoption.

Perhaps because he was adopted himself, Dave knows the value of family and understands how much we need each other. As one who has been on his own since the age of fifteen, he will tell you the word "I" is the most misunderstood and overused word in the English language.

When we are born we are the center of the universe. Our family feeds our bodies and nurtures our possibilities. All we have to do is cry and everything we want and need is brought to us.

As adolescents, we begin to learn to take care of ourselves and state our independence. We seek power. We seek control. We seek separation and identity. We try to gain a sense of self and focus on our own needs. A lot of people never outgrow this stage. If you look around, you will note there are a lot of middle-age and elderly adolescents out there.

We do not completely grow up until we learn to look beyond ourselves. We are not fully mature until we understand the truth of Dave's observation that, "When you help someone else, you are really helping yourself."

Thomas puts it this way: "You have to be able to share your success. You have to be able to give others an ownership stake and part of the rewards. People who are focused on themselves and don't share do not generally make good entrepreneurs, good employers, or good friends."

Others need us, and we need them. Everything we do is

contingent on the effort of others. "When any man of achievement stands before you," Dave Thomas says, "look closely and you will see a multitude."

The contribution others have made to our lives is reflected in all we think and do, all we believe, and all we are. Indeed, like Goethe, most of us would have to say that there would be little left of us if we were to discard what we owe to others.

QUESTION:

Make a list of the half-dozen things you most value in life. In what measure do these things result from the contributions of others?

DIVINE THUNDERBOLTS

"The moment one definitely commits oneself, then Providence moves, too. All sorts of things occur to help one that would never otherwise have occurred. Whatever you can do, or dream you can do, begin it. . . . Begin it now."

...Goethe

Until she died a couple of years ago, Hattie Williams lived on the south side of Chicago. Over the course of twenty years she had four operations for brain tumors. She was not expected to survive the first and had not recovered from the last when we met. Still, she was waiting for me on the porch when I came to interview her at her home, braced on a walker and supported by friends.

Hattie's first operation left her paralyzed and completely unable to speak. While she hovered on the edge of life she said a prayer and vowed that if she recovered, she would serve her fellow man. She did both.

For more than a quarter of a century, Hattie took care of her community, begging seed from Kmart to start gardens, obtaining permission to plant on public land, gathering and distributing clothes, organizing women's clubs and programs for teenagers, and teaching unwed mothers – whatever needed to be done.

Her couch went to a woman whose furniture had been destroyed by a fire. Her drapes became blankets to take some of the chill out of a particularly bad Chicago winter for a neighbor, and her basement became a public library. She made Christmas baskets for sixty-seven people the day before being admitted for her last surgery. When a neighbor with a newborn needed a washer, Hattie gave her own.

As word of Hattie's activities spread, people began giving her things to give away. Farmers brought her ripe tomatoes, a roomful of bread, and once a truckload of live chickens, which she kept in her house until she could distribute them to the community. Anyone who has had any significant experience with a live chicken will tell you there isn't a higher act of love than that!

I will always remember how quick she was to respond when I asked what she had learned about life. "I have learned that

God can open doors that I cannot see," Hattie said, "and that compassion is in the heart of every human being.

"When people ask for something I don't have, I just pray to the Lord and ask him to open the doors that I am unable to see," Hattie said, "and somebody calls with it."

She called the fulfillment of her prayers divine thunderbolts. For example, she said, "One of the neighbors needed a special product called Ensure. She asked if I had it, and I said, 'No, but I will pray for it.' I had never even heard of it. A week later, two cases came. We had never had it before or since.

"Another time, some of the boys wanted football uniforms for the church team and they thought maybe I knew some white people who could buy them for us. And I said to them, 'All white people are not rich, but we have a God who has everything.' We prayed to him for the uniforms and then I went upstairs to go to bed."

Before she could get to sleep, the phone rang. On the other end was a man in Elgin, Illinois, who called to say his school had just gotten new football uniforms. He said they were going to throw away or burn the old uniforms until the thought came that Hattie might have some use for them. "All we had to do was buy chin straps," she said with a smile.

Shortly after I met Hattie I got a thunderbolt of my own. In preparation for our first national awards ceremony I went to New York looking for something to signify the award. We had given a crystal dove to Mother Teresa not long before, and I had my mind set on something similar. I spent the day searching all the famous glass houses in Manhattan looking for just the right thing. Though I saw many beautiful things, nothing seemed right. I returned home disappointed.

The following morning at 10:30 the phone rang and somebody asked me to tell him about the awards. I described what we were trying to do and told him honestly about my experience in New York the day before. My new friend listened patiently to my story and then said, "Do you mind if I take a shot at it?"

"Who are you?" I said with some surprise.

"I am Frank Eliscu," he responded in a way that indicated I should know the name.

I did not and said so. "Well," he said, "I designed the Heisman Trophy about sixty years ago. I was seventeen at the time. I also designed the Presidential Eagle in the Oval Office, the Medal of Freedom, the Cascade of Books at the Library of Congress, and a number of other things you might know."

I said, "Take a shot at it, Frank."

I have since come to understand how Frank heard about us, but I still cannot explain how he happened to call when he did or why he felt the urge to volunteer for the job. There is no explanation other than to borrow Hattie's phrase and say it was a divine thunderbolt.

I have had many such experiences since that time, and so have most of those interviewed for this book. Bea Gaddy, the founder of the Patterson Park Emergency Food Center, puts it this way: "Weird things happen. I came from church one day and I found I needed tomato paste. I was doing a dinner and I didn't have one can. I said, 'Lord, if I only had tomato paste now.' In a few minutes, somebody knocked on the door. My assistant answered it and came back shaking his head. He said, 'You're not going to believe this.' There were two boxes and in each box were four or five cans of tomato paste.

"Another time a lady walked in and said she needed two thousand dollars to bury her son," Bea added. "Everybody wanted to cry because we couldn't help her. We didn't have one hundred dollars between us. In a few minutes, here comes two thousand in the mail. It seems like something always happens."

Divine thunderbolts are the markers that come out of nowhere, the validators that say you are traveling down the right path, the reminders that we are not alone. They are faith's reward.

QUESTIONS:

Has there been a time when you were at an impasse in your life and faith opened a door you could not see? Have you experienced a divine thunderbolt?

Radiate
God's Love

"When you look at the inner workings of electrical things," Mother Teresa has said, "often you see small and big wires – new and old, cheap and expensive – lined up. Until the current passes through them there will be no light. That wire is you and me. The current is God. We have the power to let the current pass through us, to use us, to produce the light of the world."

How is the light expressed? In some it is expressed in a clap of thunder and a flash of lightning. In others, you see a steady glow that builds and burns more brightly with duration. It is the response of the truth inside to the challenge of the moment. It builds each time we are thoughtful and kind, each time we seek to help and heal, each time we care. The light within us dims each time we see and do not act. It begins to die every time an act of love is lost in our indifference. Each time we walk away, the world grows dark and cold.

The Purpose of Celebrity

"A celebrity serves himself or herself. A hero goes out and redeems society."

...Joseph Campbell

If you are a fan of pro football, you probably know Mel Blount. Over fourteen years with the Pittsburgh Steelers, he participated in six consecutive championships and four Super Bowls. He led the league in interceptions in 1975 and holds the Steelers record for most interceptions in a career. He has been called the greatest athlete the game has ever seen and still stands as the standard for a defensive back.

Somewhere along the way as he became more and more successful, he began to consider the purpose of celebrity and the value of success. "Everywhere I went, the kids came up to me for my autograph," he says. "Finally, I realized they were seeking more than autographs. They were seeking attention. They were seeking recognition."

Blount was born on a farm in rural Georgia, the youngest of eleven children. He is proud to remember the circumstances of his birth and the struggles of his family during the difficult times. He's not proud of what he has, or even of what he has done, but rather of the man his background molded him to be.

"My parents are responsible for making me who I am today, because they instilled in me the right values – the importance of loving people, the importance of respecting human life and behaving responsibly. These are the basics.

Whenever life gets tough, if you have the basics, you are going to survive. It's the same way with a building. The foundation is the most important part."

Mel remembers praying with his family every Sunday morning, and working beside his parents picking cotton and growing tobacco, and he knows the difference it made in his life. "I guarantee you," he says, "if I were a kid growing up right now in some of these cities the way these kids are, I would be in all kinds of trouble. That's why my philosophy is to just let these kids experience what I experienced as a child."

The kids he is talking about are the young people who inhabit the Mel Blount Youth Homes, which are one last stop short of the penitentiary. "The kids here are under twenty-four-hour supervision," he explains. "Their days begin at the crack of dawn where they do chores like any farm boy. Then they have a normal school day. In the afternoon, they have recreational time and exercise programs. At night, they study and engage in counseling sessions.

"What we are doing is trying to mold and shape a young man the best we can in the time that we have. It's a challenge to get to these kids. It's a challenge to keep them focused. It's a challenge to get them to trust you. Most of these kids have a lot of reasons that they shouldn't trust because they come from very difficult backgrounds.

"Basically, it all comes down to one simple thing," Mel Blount says, "and that is love – having love for people and love for life. These kids will be adults someday. Hopefully, you can pass some of that on to them."

When you ask Mel how he wants to be remembered, he won't talk to you about Super Bowl rings or team records. He will say that he simply would like to be remembered as a good man. While the highlights of his football career will always be with him, the greatest satisfaction he has received is from what he has given. "There is no way to describe the happiness that comes from within and the peace that comes when you see you have really touched a young life in a positive way.

"I now know that regardless of what I have, whether it is a million dollars in the bank or farms and cattle, horses, a big reputation, or whatever, God just gives you those things to use. When I die, those things are going to be left here for somebody else to use. You really don't own anything in this world. What matters is what you do with what you are given."

QUESTION:

As Mel Blount points out, many kids are growing up in a challenging environment. How strong is your family's foundation?

A WORLD OF POSSIBILITIES

"We are all of us angels with only one wing. We can only fly while embracing each other."

...Luciano de Crescenzo

Every nook and cranny of Leeanne McGrath's suburban home and two-car garage is filled with items in transition. Though she has given what she does a name – The Sharing Connection – there is no budget, no office, no board of directors, or no official job positions. Leeanne, the founder and the driving force behind the Connection, prefers all volunteers to be known simply as helpers.

"We are all amateurs," Leeanne says. "We are all learners. And I think that's part of the beauty of this. Other agencies do need a staff. They do need a budget. But we work with what we have and all of us are just giving our time. So any dollar that's given goes right into what is needed at that moment. And I have to tell you that it's like the multiplication of the loaves and fishes."

More than a dozen years ago, Leeanne began transforming her house into a collection and redistribution center for food and clothing, furniture, toiletries, and baby items like toys and cribs. Now she helps support some three dozen homeless shelters, food pantries, and other service organizations in and around Chicago.

Goods are collected from her home by the truckload five days a week. The garage is always left open so that anyone can sign in and take what they need. McGrath's mission is simple. She is a "bridge between caring people and people who need care."

It began with the Crib Project. While volunteering at Marillac House in Chicago's inner city, she was told, "If you can provide a crib, you can save a life." Without a crib, infants are at risk in the unprotected areas of tenement housing.

"I came home with that challenge," Leeanne recalls. "Find a crib and save a life. I didn't know if we'd ever be able find one, but I was determined to try." Nine years later, McGrath has found and donated 678 cribs to those in need.

Each crib is outfitted with linens, bumpers, a baby afghan, and a teddy bear.

As McGrath's work with Chicago's needy grew, she began serving as a liaison between food suppliers and food service agencies in the Chicago area. She made arrangements with local farmers for food service agencies to pick up their extra produce at the end of the day. Now she begins each day with a phone call at 4:30 A.M. to see what produce will be available that day. Then, she and other volunteers make the rounds and deliver the goods to those agencies that don't have their own transportation.

As winter approaches McGrath involves local cleaners in an annual winter coat drive. In addition to providing a convenient location to receive the coats, the Laundromats clean all the coats before McGrath distributes them. She distributes over a thousand coats a year.

When McGrath first began her work with The Sharing Connection, she thought she would have to travel across town to find people in need. She soon learned she didn't have to venture far. She found poverty and hunger existed in her own neighborhood. She also found she could have a global impact out of her living room.

"I never thought we would be able to reach across an ocean," Leeanne says with wonder. "But we have." McGrath and her friends have gathered and donated everything from paint for orphanages in Mexico; shoes for children in Russia; twenty-two thousand pounds of medical equipment and clothing for Romanians; medical supplies, toys, and clothing for the people of Bosnia; and sewing machines and medical supplies for Haiti.

"She moves mountains," one of her volunteers said, "one grain at a time."

"I believe in just sharing the possibilities," Leeanne said, "and letting other people come up with their own answers. So whenever I speak to a group, I suggest that they go home and just think about it and let it rest on their heart. If I asked for something specific, I would never know what the possibilities are.

"One woman said, 'Oh, I don't want to talk about this; this is so depressing.' I said, 'Please stay and finish the conversation, because I don't see it as depressing. I hope that you will feel as excited as I do about the things we can do to help each other.'

"When I began, if I am really honest, I have to tell you it was a selfish need. I was reading stories in the newspaper and it made me so distressed. You can't help thinking the problems are so vast, and if you let yourself, you *can* get depressed. You sit and do nothing and feel hopeless and helpless. But I have found it so much more wonderful to consider the possibilities, to ask yourself the question – I wonder if there is anything we can do to help – to think of all the big or little things you can do and learn that together we can make a difference.

"All I know is I can't stop. It's become a way of life. I think I'd become very sad if I couldn't do this. When you know the need, it's hard to walk away from it."

QUESTION:

Take Leeanne's challenge. Let it rest on your heart. What possibilities do you see?

CARING IS CONTAGIOUS

"Modern man's greatest problems stem from his loss
of any sense of meaningful participating with God in
His purposes for mankind."

...Dostoevski

"We live our lives between a desire for security and a yearning
for fulfillment," Jack McConnell says. "We aspire to a full life
but refuse to release the old and discover the new. We are like
the trapeze artist swaying on the perch, high above the seats in
a circus tent, hesitating to grab the swing when it comes to
him, and so, the act comes to an end.

"The only way to find a full life," he says, "is to reach out
to others." To illustrate his point he describes his understanding of the biblical story of the loaves and fishes.

"There are three possible explanations," McConnell
explains. "One, we may regard it simply as a miracle. Two, it
may be a sacramental meal, where each of the five thousand
people present was given but a morsel. Or, three, there may be
a more captivating explanation:

"Who among us would leave on a very long walk with no
preparation for food?" he asks. "The miracle occurred near
the Feast of Passover. If there were pilgrims among those present, they undoubtedly would possess supplies sufficient for
the trip."

But perhaps none of them was willing to share, McConnell
speculates. When Jesus produced the very ordinary barley

loaves and the pitifully small amount of fish, perhaps everyone who had food was moved by this example. Everyone shared, and in the end there was enough, more than enough, for everyone.

"Perhaps the miracle has less to do with the division of limited food supplies and more with the multiplication of those who care enough to share, less with turning water into wine and more with teaching those whose instinct is to keep how to give."

Jack McConnell is not a pastor, but he is one of seven children born to a pastor in the coal mining region of West Virginia. From his humble beginnings he went on to become one of the most respected physicians in the country. During his medical career, McConnell led the development teams that invented the TB Tyne test, Tylenol, and the MRI. Most recently, he has been heavily involved in The Genome Project, the hugely successful effort to map human genes.

When he retired to Hilton Head, South Carolina, he expected to spend his time playing golf and relaxing. Instead, he found himself drawn to the desperate conditions he saw on "the other side" of the island. "We live in what some would consider a wealthy housing development and yet when you go out the back exit, you drive into abject poverty. An enormous chasm exists between the two worlds on the island, separated by a simple fence."

As he drove out the back gate McConnell wondered how the island's eight to ten thousand working poor could afford good medical care. On New Year's Day in 1992, McConnell came up with the idea of a free clinic. Within days, he began enlisting others who could help him realize his dream. In his vision, retired physicians, nurses, dentists, and lay people would volunteer to provide free care to medically underserved people.

"I think the project started the same way that Robert Frost says every poem starts – with a lump in the throat," McConnell said. He knew it would work when at the first meeting he called to discuss the project, sixteen physicians volunteered to work at the clinic – if he could get it off the ground.

McConnell was able to persuade the South Carolina legislature to pass a bill directing the Board of Medical Examiners to create a special Volunteer License, which allowed retired physicians to practice medicine at the clinic without having take the state's licensing exam. He also persuaded the legislature to extend the Good Samaritan Law to the clinic volunteers, obtained unlimited malpractice insurance for clinic volunteers, and raised the capital needed to construct the clinic – over $1 million – from within the local community.

McConnell next set out to recruit retired medical professionals and lay people to help staff the clinic. He recruited more than 54 physicians, 57 nurses, 4 dentists, and 150 lay volunteers.

The clinic, called Volunteers in Medicine, began operating on a part-time basis in the spring of 1993. In June 1994, the clinic was debt-free and operating full hours. To date, the clinic has seen over ten thousand patients for a total of twenty-five thousand patient visits.

In caring for the poor, Dr. McConnell noted the clinic also fulfilled a need for the "wealthy" half of the island. "We had many retired physicians, nurses, and dentists who found playing golf and tennis less fulfilling than they had expected. The creation of the VIM Clinic helped add purpose to their lives.

"Caring is contagious," he says. "I have letter after letter from physicians and nurses who say when I retired I thought I had the world by the tail, going to play a lot of golf and tennis and travel and play some bridge. And after six months, eighteen months, they all say the same thing – I had a hole inside of me that wasn't being filled by what I was doing.

"We have at the outset two individuals, one well off and one not so well off. At the end we have two people bonded in a moment of sharing and caring. It is there that the healing occurs."

To illustrate his point, Jack recalls the three-year-old girl who wandered away from her house into the fields in Iowa where her parents were working. They soon missed her and called, but she did not respond. They started a search immediately but could not find her. They called neighbors, scattered across the farm, and looked without success for two days.

Finally, someone suggested they join hands and march across the fields together. They did and found the little girl – dead. "The mother's poignant question still haunts me," he said. "She said, 'Why didn't we join hands before?'

"That's what we are doing at the clinic. It is transforming the lives of the friends and neighbors, the lives of the volunteers, and, by extension, transforming our town into a community," said McConnell. "No town can become a community as long as we leave behind a segment of the population in need of the basics of life."

The vision statement of the clinic says it all. It reads: "May we have eyes to see those who are rendered invisible and excluded, open arms and hearts to reach out and include them, healing hands to touch their lives with love, and, in the process, heal ourselves."

QUESTIONS:

Who are the invisible ones in your community? How can you personally reach out to them?

OUR BEST EX-PRESIDENT

"One of the difficulties with all our institutions is the fact that we've emphasized the reward instead of the service."

...Harry S. Truman

Regardless of political persuasion, most people will readily agree that Jimmy Carter is our best ex-president. While others have retired from Washington and the White House to rest and reflect, profit and play, President Carter has consistently sought new ways to serve and benefit society.

The Carters spent ten years on center stage, then returned to private life in Georgia in 1981. There they considered what to do next.

"One night I woke up and Jimmy was sitting straight up in bed, which was very unusual," Rosalynn Carter recalls. "I thought he was sick and I asked, 'What's the matter?' He said, 'I know what we can do at The Carter Center. We can have a place to resolve conflict. If there had been such a place, I wouldn't have had to take Begin and Sadat to Camp David."

The Carter Center in Atlanta was designed with that in mind. It includes the Jimmy Carter Library, Global 2000 Inc., the Task Force on Child Survival and Development, and the Carter-Menil Human Rights Foundation.

For Carter, "human rights" is a broad term. "I think peace is a basic human right," he has said. "Environmental quality, democracy, and freedom are human rights." Through Global 2000, The Carter Center has initiated disease control and large-scale agricultural projects in Ghana, Zambia, Sudan, Nigeria, Pakistan, and China. The Center has led in nearly eradicating the disease called Guinea One, and it is targeting other diseases that can be prevented and controlled globally. The Task Force for Child Survival sets up immunization and other child survival projects in developing countries.

At first most of the work of The Carter Center was overseas, but one day, Rosalynn remembers, "Jimmy came in and said, 'You know what we are going to do? We are going to try to solve all the human problems in Atlanta.' He said he had been feeling guilty because he had been working so hard overseas, while we had some of the same problems in our country."

The result – the Atlanta Project – is an unprecedented, communitywide effort to attack the social problems associated with poverty in urban areas. This grassroots effort calls upon volunteers, at least ninety-three thousand to date, to work with residents in twenty communities to identify needs and create avenues for change.

As part of their personal commitment, President and Mrs. Carter have helped build at least one home for someone in need each year for twelve years.

When you meet the Carters, the impression you get is of people who are very down to earth, more like your neighbor than Washingtonians. They seem happier in Plains than they ever were in the White House. You get the impression that they were never completely comfortable with all the pomp and pretentiousness of the political world and that they serve because it is in their natures to serve.

If you ask him, Jimmy will say he would like to be remembered "as someone who was committed to the strengthening of human rights." I suspect Carter's purpose and place in history will be better served by a thousand small acts of kindness and consideration than by all of his presidential global initiatives. I suspect the Carters will be remembered more for what they have done personally than for what they have done politically. Few people can leave the pinnacle of power and ascend to even greater heights.

QUESTIONS:
Which recent political leader do you most admire? Why? Is their character such that you would find it admirable in a neighbor? Would you want your children to follow their example?

IV BE THE LIGHT

"THE SIMPLEST WAY OF BECOMING LIGHT IS BY BEING KIND AND LOVING, THOUGHTFUL AND SINCERE WITH EACH OTHER. NEVER LET ANYONE COME TO YOU WITHOUT COMING AWAY BETTER AND HAPPIER."

...*MOTHER TERESA*

A Society Is What It Honors

President Kennedy said, "A nation reveals itself not only by the men it produces but also by the men it honors, the men it remembers." At the moment, most of the people we honor live in the toy department of life – entertainers and athletes.

There is nothing wrong with distracting and entertaining people. But you have to ask yourself – what do these people do to merit so much attention, such recognition and reward? What do they contribute to our lives that we should deify them thus? What do they do that justifies the way we glorify their name, promote their personalities, enshrine their achievement, and often excuse their antisocial behavior?

If the way we celebrate these performers reflects a belief that they have reached the pinnacle of human achievement, what does that say about us as a society? What does it say about our values? What kind of message, what kind of example are they providing for our young?

Is it enough to perfect some physical skill? Is it enough to perform well? Is it enough to remember and regurgitate your lines? Is it enough to learn how to convey emotion on demand?

I have to confess that like a lot of kids in my generation, I wanted to be Mickey Mantle. I have nothing against a basketball player, a football player, or any other athlete. Actors and actresses can be, and often are, attractive, exciting, and entertaining individuals. But neither skill nor even the perfection of their talent makes of them the stuff of heroes. What does a man who can jump high, hit the ball long, or run fast do to redeem society? It may say something about the perfection of human potential, but taken alone it is a rather flat and one-dimensional image.

Unfortunately, America's true heroes, the heroes of the heart, are less visible, but if you examine your life you will most likely find them near the center of your being. They are the parents and grandparents who reached out to us when we were children, the people who sacrificed for and sustained us, the teachers who nurtured our growth. They are known by the content of their character, not the size of their salaries or the number of their possessions.

A celebrity speaks to the surface. A hero speaks to the soul. Sometimes a man can be both. Christopher Reeve has gone from celebrity to hero.

In this distinction may lie the central issue for our society as we enter the next century. The second president of the United States, John Adams, reminds us, "Our Constitution was designed only for a moral and religious people. It is wholly inadequate for the government of any other."

The only other great democracy in the history of the world fell because, at the end, the freedom the Athenians wanted was the freedom from responsibility. Because they wanted more *from* society than they were willing to give *to* society, society dissolved and fell apart.

If American society is not to go the way of Athens, we will have to decide what our country and our lives are all about. What do we value? What conduct should we capture, encourage, and reinforce? If we are to regain the high ground and lead the world into the light, we will have to find a way to realign our values so that the actions of those we celebrate and ask our children to emulate reflect the best of ourselves and our nation.

THE KINDNESS OF STRANGERS

"America is great because America is good. America
will cease to be great when it is no longer good."

...*Alexis de Tocqueville*

John Gardner is the epitome of public service. In some way,
he has touched and benefited the lives of every citizen of
this country.

As president of the Carnegie Foundation; secretary of the
Department of Health, Education and Welfare; founder of
Common Cause and the Independent Sector; and as author,
educator, and advisor to six presidents, he has served society for
nearly fifty years. I met him at Stanford, where he spends most
of his time these days, focusing on the need for community.

For Gardner the issue of community is central to all soci-
eties and cultures because it is so much easier to be unkind to
people you don't know. "The easiest unkindness is the unkindness to people you regard as nonpersons," he observes. "They
are from the tribe in the next valley or their skin color is different or they don't speak the same language."

On delivering the centennial commencement address at
Stanford, Gardner offered this advice to the graduating class.
He did not wish them the conventional message of success, he
said, for success as the world measures it is too easy. "I wish
you something harder to come by. I would like to wish you
meaning in your life.

"The aim is that you not suffer the contemporary fate of root-
lessness, hollowness, and faithlessness, that you not succumb to

the ailment of the age – the tyranny of imperious, imprisoning self. The commitments that people make to values beyond the self are manifested in various ways in their family and community life, in the way they treat any and all humans, in the goals and standards they set for themselves. There are men and women who make the world better just by being the kind of people they are. They have the gift of kindness or courage or loyalty or integrity. It really matters very little whether they are behind the wheel of a truck or running a business or bringing up a family. They teach the truth by living it."

As the historian Alfred North Whitehead observed, "The kindness of the American people is, so far as I know, something unique in the history of the world." Many other social critics, going back to de Tocqueville, have made a similar observation.

Americans have always had a genius for splendid and unselfish action. That is the glory of America and our challenge. As Gardner concludes, "if we fail, if we fall, it will not be as a result of some external threat. Our civilization will die when we no longer care."

QUESTION:
History has proven we can justify almost any unkindness if we can sufficiently distinguish "us" from "them." Ask the Nazis. Are the poor, the homeless, or the alien nonpersons in your community?

THE CHILDREN SHALL LEAD US

"Tomorrow can be better, but only if young people help make it so. That is their mission – to make tomorrow better."

...William B. Walsh

I am old enough to remember hearing talk about the beatnik generation. Then, we sighed over the "lost" generation of hippies. After that, there was the "me" generation and the dreadful self-absorption that term suggested.

Currently we are dealing with Generation X. We have run out of names and resorted to letters.

But these dismissive titles overlook one consistent fact. If you look at the principal, positive social movements in each of those eras, it is the young people who have led.

Young people led the antiwar movement. Young people led the environmental movement and the women's movement and provided the backbone of the civil rights movement. Everywhere you look, you will find students at the forefront of liberty and justice – from Tiananmen Square to the Berlin Wall and South Africa.

The energy and idealism of our young people is our nation's greatest resource. Today, it is our young people who are driving us toward the dawn of the new age. It has been my great privilege to meet many of these young "rebels." Individually, they are remarkable. Collectively, they are an awesome group.

Though many of them are just entering their teens, what

they are about is not kids' stuff. Jason Gaes was diagnosed with cancer at the age of six and told, odds were, he would never see seven. Jason battled and beat the disease and then, at the age of eight, wrote a book about his experience to help other kids who were fighting cancer, too.

Jason said he wanted a book with a happy ending, because all the books he read while he was sick were so scary. He included his phone number in the book in case anyone wanted his help. Since then, he has responded to over twelve thousand phone calls and made hundreds of appearances around the country.

Though he has yet to graduate from college, Nick Walters has already raised three quarter of a million dollars for juvenile diabetes. Melissa Helmbrecht, who nearly flunked out of school until she found herself in helping others, helped start a charter school for at-risk children in Trenton before going off to law school in Denver this fall. Melissa is a frequent lecturer, student leader, and author of a new book on domestic violence.

Melissa Poe began her crusade to clean up the environment at the age of eight. At eleven, Trevor Ferrell opened his own shelter for the homeless. Amber Coffman started her program for the homeless when she was eight years old. Seven-year-old Emily Kumpel filled a library in South Africa with books, then started a service program for kids at the age of eight, and by nine had her own radio program. When I called for her a year ago, I was somewhat taken aback to hear that this eleven-year-old couldn't come to the phone because she was busy interviewing Desmond Tutu.

Mariah Sharkey created solidarity at Yuba City High School in California. Modeled after Lech Walesa's Solidarity

Movement in Poland, her goal was to bring people together, reminding them of their commonalties while celebrating their diversity and differences. The program was such a success that it has been copied and implemented at twenty-five California high schools and is having an impact on over fifty thousand students a year.

During the summer of her junior year, Jody Wiatt decided it was time to change the reputation of her high school. She didn't like the empty emphasis of the school's social clubs and came up with the idea of starting the Mustang Memorial Outreach Bunch, the MMOB.

Starting with fifteen members, the MMOB began simply with a trip to visit residents of a local nursing home. From there the activities of the MMOB grew exponentially. Members planted seeds for a local food pantry, tutored elementary school kids, initiated a "buddy" system for special ed students to make them feel welcome, organized painting projects, and helped rehabilitate housing.

Entirely student led and directed, the MMOB under Jody's leadership grew to be the biggest organization in the school. By the time she graduated, a fifth of the student body belonged. The program still continues, five years after her graduation.

"The trick is to help kids understand it's cool to care," Jody said. "When kids can do things like this, when they can find a way to make things better not only for themselves and other kids, but for a lot of adults as well, it is so empowering. After a while, you feel like you can do anything."

Chad Perlyn created Doc-Adopt, persuading 120 physicians to donate free services to needy children, "adopting" them medically. Though still a teen, Chad succeeded where the local medical association had failed and was called on to give them guidance on how to make a broader program work.

"I was raised with an understanding of my personal responsibility to act," Chad says. "I was expected and I expect myself to recognize the pain in other people and to do something about it."

It is a sentiment shared by all of the good young people I have come to know over the last fifteen years. They realize that everything begins with one person.

Mariah Sharkey spoke for all of them when she said, quoting Eli Wiesel, "But where do I start? The world is so vast, I shall start with the country I know best, my own. But my country, too, is so very large. I had better start with my town. Large also is my town. I had best start with my street. No, my home. No, my family. Never mind, I shall start with myself."

QUESTION:

A recent survey found that only 37 percent of all Americans believe the children of today will make the world a better place. If you are not among them, if you are not optimistic about the future, what are you doing to help the children turn their world around?

A PROFILE IN COURAGE

"One can give nothing whatsoever without giving oneself – that is to say, risking oneself. If one cannot risk
oneself, then one is simply incapable of giving."

...James Baldwin

Almost a half century ago, former President Kennedy wrote a Pulitzer Prize-winning book that described the political courage of some of our best and brightest. These were men who sailed against the tide, risking their careers and political fortunes for a principle.

That was a departure, for its time, from the traditional notion of courage. Then and now we tend to associate courage with danger: a firefighter rushing into a burning building to rescue a child, a soldier in battle, or some other act of heroism. Rarely do we applaud the courage of kindness, the strength of selflessness and service.

While they are not as celebrated as the political leaders President Kennedy described, some of our young people today could teach them a thing or two about the nature of real courage. Consider Henry Nicols, for example, and ask yourself which is more remarkable – to lay your career on the line for a principle, or your life?

Fifteen years ago, Henry, a hemophiliac, tested HIV-positive. He was ten years old. The discovery came in the wake of the Ryan White affair. Ryan, who had also tested positive under similar circumstances, was driven out of school when his family went public with his situation and was subjected to a great deal of abuse.

Understandably concerned about the consequences disclosure would have on Henry's life, his family decided to keep his condition secret. But Henry chose another course. He decided to tell the community about his condition.

Henry wanted to help his community overcome their fears and prejudices about AIDS and AIDS victims. He was tired of hearing the jokes about AIDS. He wanted to warn his classmates, the highest risk group for AIDS, of the consequences of their risky sexual behavior. They never dreamed they could contract this disease. He was willing to risk rejection, fear, anger, and ignorance in order to be of service.

The word *courage* comes from a French word meaning heart. It takes a lot of heart to care enough to put yourself at risk of such rejection. Henry began where it was most difficult, telling his peers at high school. Since then Henry has made presentations concerning AIDS to over a thousand schools across the country. Henry has appeared on talk shows and was featured in *Parade* and in a special on HBO.

He now averages two or three presentations a week and feels like he is beginning to get his message across. "Teenagers react completely differently," he says, "when they get the message from another teen."

What Henry has been able to do is among the most difficult of things. He has opened people's minds, touched their hearts, and made them think. In the process he has undoubtedly saved hundreds of lives.

"It is curious," Mark Twain said, "that physical courage should be so common in the world, and moral courage so rare." Henry Nicols defines the word. When he was honored for his commitment to others, Henry accepted his award by announcing his candidacy for president. I was among those who laughed at the eighteen-year-old boy's statement. We all stopped laughing when Henry pointed out that, in order to run, he would first have to survive longer than any other AIDS victim on record. He knows if he can do that, the rest will be comparatively easy. When he is ready, I plan to be his campaign manager.

QUESTIONS:

Which would you applaud more in your children, physical courage or moral courage? Which have you applauded most recently?

The Key to Happiness

All you have to do is look at the tabloids to know that some of the wealthiest people in America are among the most miserable human beings on earth.

Money can't buy happiness, nor can fame guarantee it. One of the more ironic and common aspects of sudden celebrity is the rapid fleeing of what has been so avidly pursued. After years of doing whatever possible to draw attention to themselves, new stars begin seeking every opportunity to withdraw, disguising their appearance, hiding their eyes behind sunglasses, and often bitterly complaining when they can't appear in public without being noticed.

Life circumstances, such as salary, education, and marital status, are no greater indicators of happiness. Studies conducted by researchers at the University of Minnesota confirmed this fact. "Those in prestigious positions or professions were not happier than those who went to work in overalls, nor were those who finished their Ph.D.'s happier than those who never completed the eighth grade," Dr. Auke Tellegran, one of the coauthors of the study, reported.

Nor is happiness determined by race, geography, or religion.

The people profiled in this book cross all these social boundaries. Some have great resources. Others have very modest means. If fact, it's safe to say that probably the only thing they have in common is their commitment to serve others – and the happiness that results.

"My life is a good life," Mother Hale, the humble founder of Hale House in Harlem told me. "If I go to sleep tonight and don't get up tomorrow I know it's been a good day and I have done something for somebody. I really and truly feel good. I love every day and every night of the eighty-six years that I have had on this earth. I wouldn't trade it for anybody."

Harriet Hodges, known as the "Angel in a Jeep" during World War II and subsequently as the "Queen of Hearts" for her work in Korea, agrees. "When I think back, I don't remember when I won this or when I did that," she said. "I think of this person or that child I helped and that is the most satisfying thing in life to me."

Ferdinand Mahfood, the businessman who founded Food for the Poor, says, "If people could understand that greatness comes from serving others, then a lot of happiness would come into this country. There are a lot of very wealthy Americans that are very unhappy people because they are looking for happiness by getting other people to serve them."

God has so constituted our nature that we cannot be happy unless we are useful to others. The most miserable people on earth must be those who feel that they are not needed and they have no purpose. The walls of incapacity and self-absorption, like the walls of prison, separate. They leave us empty, wretched, and alone.

THE HAPPIEST LAWYER IN THE WORLD

"One thing I know – the only ones among you who will be really happy are those who have sought and found how to serve."

...Albert Schweitzer

There are four things about Nancy Mintie that make her a most unusual lawyer: She has never lost a case. She doesn't make a lot of money. She doesn't like the law. And she is happy.

"I had no intrinsic interest in law as a discipline," Mintie recalls of her career decision. "To me it's more like plumbing. It's a tool to fix things. Other than that, I have to confess it doesn't do a thing for me. I'm bored silly by the law in and of itself."

Though she had no specific interest in law, Nancy brought to her practice a passion for justice. As a young child she remembers reading biographies of people who had worked for social change and feeling like she was on fire.

After graduating from law school, Nancy set up an office in the inner city of Los Angeles. Lacking capital, she traded labor in a soup kitchen for space in an adjacent garage. Mornings, she worked in the soup kitchen. Afternoons, she practiced law. Often people followed her directly from one to the other, bringing their papers and their problems with them.

From the beginning, it was a hand-to-mouth operation. To this day, some fifteen years later, The Inner City Law Center, Nancy's firm, still cannot claim more than a month's reserve.

But in the meantime, her practice has grown to average three thousand clients a year – many of them the poorest of the poor.

Nancy's practice deals with all the urgent life and health issues, but through the years the Center has developed a special expertise in slum housing litigation. "The kind of housing conditions we have dealt with through the years have been abominable," she says. "We've had children die in these buildings, a pregnant woman who lost her child because of a miscarriage after being bitten by a rat, and all kinds of other terrible conditions."

To illustrate her point, Mintie talks of the Ramirez family, a family of five occupying two rooms in a run-down apartment building. "When I went in there I saw a place that looked like it had been scrubbed within an inch of its life," she says, "then I noticed the little girl's dolls were in plastic bags and hung up on the wall. When I asked why, the mother said 'the rats eat them if we don't bag them that way.'"

Mrs. Ramirez went on to describe what it was like living in a building overrun by rats and cockroaches. She told Mintie the ceiling had recently collapsed on a neighbor. The building was so unsafe two children had been sexually assaulted on the premises and a boy had fallen through the stairwell.

Outraged, Nancy filed suit and took the landlord to the cleaners. She takes great satisfaction in telling you how the case ending up with a huge settlement the eve of the trial, and the difference it made in her clients' lives. Some of the families bought their first home with the money. Others started businesses, became self-sufficient, and sent their kids to school.

"After that I would walk down the street and people would elbow each other and say, 'Hey, that's my lawyer. There goes my lawyer,'" Nancy says with obvious delight, "and I really loved that, because that was my greatest desire – to be a lawyer for the poor."

The reason doctors, lawyers, and priests have traditionally been held in high esteem is that they helped people. They provided a service that was valuable. Lately, the credibility of all these professionals has suffered. Instead of serving others, they are often perceived as serving their own interests and putting themselves first.

For these troubled souls, Nancy suggests, "You have to ask yourself why you do it? What makes you happy? What brings you peace and comfort? For me, it's always been the ability to engage in some kind of compassionate action. I feel I must be the happiest lawyer in the world."

QUESTIONS:
What makes you happy? If you haven't found happiness in your career, what can you do that will bring you nearer your goal?

LIFESTYLES OF THE RICH AND FAMOUS

"Joy is not in things. It is in us."

...Richard Wagner

"I occasionally watch *Lifestyles of the Rich and Famous*," Mitzi Perdue says, "mostly to giggle. I can't help thinking those guys are nuts. They're missing what gives life meaning and purpose."

Mitzi should know better than most. She is the wife of Frank Perdue of Perdue Chickens, one of the largest privately held companies in the country, and the daughter of one of the founders of Sheraton Hotels. "When you get right down to it, I like jewelry," she adds. "It's pretty. But so what? These material things are awfully nice but they don't bring happiness. They don't bring satisfaction. I think I'd be bored stiff with the jet-set stuff. It's not real. It's ephemeral. It has no consequence."

Mitzi's lifestyle is one you won't see on the *Rich and Famous*, but you probably should. She lives with her family in a modest house in rural Maryland. There are no hoards of servants around, no lavish cars, no extravagant decorations. I doubt if there is a single solid gold faucet on the premises.

Rather than taking long vacations in the Caribbean or on the Riviera, Mitzi prefers to devote her time to her community and to the welfare of kids. "I guess in life you make choices," she explains. "You spend your time and allocate it where you get the greatest reward. Selfishly, I have chosen to do things that impact positively on other people's lives. That's what makes me happy.

"When I'm really unhappy, I try to stand aside a little bit and think, am I wishing for something that's not coming my way? Am I wanting to take? Almost always, when I'm unhappy, it's when the motive is 'somebody owes me something.'"

To support her argument, Mitzi points to a biography of Napoléon she has just finished reading. "Napoléon conquered the world, but near the end of his life he wrote in his diary that he only had five happy days in his entire life. Contrast that with Mother Teresa. She eats the bread of the poor, only owns three cotton saris and her sandals, and lives a life of poverty. Yet, she describes her life as a feast of unending joy."

One of Mitzi's chief sources of satisfaction is derived from a program she helped start for young people called Youth Engaged in Service (YES). The program is now in over one hundred schools in a dozen states.

"I was looking for some force that would bring more joy to kids' lives than Nike sneakers," she says, "and I think community service is the answer. To me the function of YES is inspiration, and the more of it, the better. To me inspiration is the greatest gift one person can give another because it gives you a road map of where to go and it gives you the energy to get there."

Despite what you have seen on TV, she concludes, "Success is not measured by what you can get. Success is measured by what you give. Whatever step anybody takes, no matter how small, it is valuable because it brings us closer to a better world."

QUESTIONS:

Who is the happiest person you know? What is their secret?

A HAPPY DEATH

"We have committed The Golden Rule to memory; let us now commit it to life."

...Edwin Markham

Arthur Flemming died last year. He was ninety-three.

I have many memories of Arthur through the years, but the one that will stay with me the longest is the last. When I visited him in the hospital shortly before he died, I was struck by how relaxed and at peace he was. There was no impatience and aggravation in this man who, up until only a few days before, had kept one of the busiest calendars in Washington. There was no fear or frustration. Arthur was at peace.

How did a man who spent his career in politics achieve that peace, that knowledge that he had lived a good life? He simply lived as a public servant. Many politicians who serve themselves instead of the people have turned that term into an oxymoron, but Arthur knew, in the words of John Quincy Adams, that "private interests must not be put in opposition to public good."

Arthur served six presidents, chaired the U.S. Civil Rights Commission, and was president of three colleges. In that time his highest public salary was twenty-five thousand dollars.

The first president that Arthur met was Coolidge. The first president he served was Roosevelt, the last was Reagan, and he served every president in between. Though he held no office when he died, he was still called on for advice by President Clinton, who awarded Arthur the Medal of Freedom in 1994.

Arthur served on the Civil Service Commission, the War Manpower Commission, and the Labor Management Commission. He ran the Office of Defense Mobilization during World War II, and served as the youngest member of the Hoover Commission.

President Eisenhower appointed him to serve on the Committee on Government Organization, the National Security Council, the second Hoover Commission and, finally, made him Secretary of the Department of Health Education and Welfare.

Kennedy appointed him to the committee that developed what is now known as Medicare. Nixon appointed him to head the White House Conference on Aging and made him U.S. Commissioner on Aging as well as Chairman of the U.S. Civil Rights Commission. Flemming served in this capacity through the Ford, Carter, and into the Reagan administrations. He continued to be active in areas of health and Social Security as head of the Save Our Security coalition he cofounded with former Secretary Wilbur Cohen.

In five decades of public service, there was never a scandal attached to his name and he never engaged in partisanship. Though a life-long Republican, he served Democrats and Republicans alike. He has tried to live his life true to his belief that public service is the highest calling on earth.

"The commandment – thou shall love they neighbor as thyself – has always meant a great deal to me," he said, "though at times I was troubled by doubts of my ability to fully execute it. I was helped by the interpretation of a pastor I heard in London during the war."

The pastor said that the commandment imposes no

obligation upon people to "like" their neighbor. "I breathed a sigh of relief when I heard that," Arthur said, "because I knew a few people I found hard to like." The important thing is to love all of humanity.

"I have tried to keep the Second Commandment at the center of my thinking," Arthur said. "In the areas where we have the opportunity of contact with our fellow human beings, it seems to me that we have this obligation, this common responsibility, to help our neighbor achieve her or his highest possibility."

Given this, it is not surprising that Arthur's favorite public position was secretary of HEW. "Every morning when you woke up, you knew you had the opportunity to do something during the day that would help a number of people," he said. "Sometimes it would be several hundred and sometimes several million, but always someone. I could hardly wait to get to work."

When Arthur knew he was dying, he had the peace of a man who knows he has done all he can, used every opportunity, given all he was given to benefit his fellow man. Such is a happy death. It is the death of no regrets, the death without end.

QUESTION:

As we age, our bodies become nothing more than wilted leaves on the tree of life, but the energy we have spent remains. If you were to die tomorrow, would it be a happy death?

The Secret
of Success

Benjamin Franklin said, "It is a great mistake to think of being great without goodness; and I pronounce it as certain that there was never yet a truly great man that was not at the same time truly virtuous." By that measure, Rachel Rossow is more successful than Donald Trump. Momma Hawk is more successful than Madonna, and Millard Fuller is more successful than Michael Jackson.

The success of Trump, Madonna, and Jackson is tangible, while the success of Rachel, Momma Hawk, and Millard is intangible, less visible, and more real.

Trump, like a lot of businessmen, measures his success by the size of his portfolio, the number of corporations he controls, and how far up the Fortune 500 he climbs. Madonna and Michael Jackson keep score by the number of records they sell and the size of their fan clubs.

Millard measures his success in families sheltered and people fed. Rachel's and Momma Hawk's contributions have been made to the children, their comfort and education. These good and wise people have invested their time in the currents of life. Their contribution will remain long after the records have fallen, the gold is gone, and Trump's empire has collapsed.

The secret to success starts with a full understanding of what life is about and why we are here. In the words of Martin Luther King, Jr., "Every person must feel responsibility to discover his mission in life. God has given each person capacity to achieve some end. True, some are endowed with more talent than others, but God has left none of us talentless."

Ours is an age marked by the perfection of means and a confusion of ends. Most of our education is dedicated to the perfection of skills without considering their application. Once we have discovered and perfected our talents, we must work assiduously to discover the ends for which they were designed.

What is your mission in life? Where might your talents prove most useful? Our success is measured by the degree to which we employ our gifts in the service of others.

The Saint of South Carolina

"Man should not consider his material possessions his own, but as common to all, so as to share them without hesitation when others are in need."

...Saint Thomas Aquinas

John Fling is the only man I have ever met who completely and consistently responds to the challenge of Aquinas. For fifty years – all of his adult life – he has given everything away – everything he has made, everything he has been given.

The clothes he gives away are often better than the clothes he wears. He doesn't own a television, but he has purchased several for others. He doesn't own a car and has never owned a home, but he has helped many people buy theirs.

John lives in a cottage behind his mother-in-law's house. Although he has worked all his life, all he has to his name is five thousand dollars in the bank, and that's to cover funeral expenses for himself or his wife.

All he does is whatever needs doing for an extended family that includes four hundred children, two hundred seniors, and about forty blind people. Every day John Fling goes looking for someone else to help. He buys food, delivers food and laundry, transports the needy to medical appointments, and responds to dozens of calls from people in need.

He helps the elderly with the medicine they need, pays the rent when cash is short, or helps with the utility bills, especially gas and electricity. "If the refrigerator or the air conditioning goes out," he says, "that's a real problem. Older people suffer in this heat."

"The blind people like to get out," Fling says. He takes them to the beach or out to the lake to go fishing.

Fling grew up on the banks of the Chattahoochee River. "Our family was so poor," he says, "we weren't even share-croppers. We were sharecropper's helpers. What we ate, we had to catch out of the water, dig out of the ground, or shake out of a tree."

Fling is unincorporated and refuses to form an organization. There is no board to direct him, no committee to support his activities. He never begs, has never held a fund-raiser, and never even asked for help. "I don't ever ask for anything," he says. "I don't do anything to promote my activities. If somebody wants to help me, I will accept it, but I don't ask for it. My billfold is a lot of times empty, but when I've got it, I use it."

Fling's crusade began when he took a job that required him to supervise children selling newspapers on the street. "When you have seventy-five to a hundred children with you all day, you are going to know where they live," he says. "You are going to know who they live with and you are going to know their needs."

Half a century later, Fling still knows what children need. They emerge magically at the sound of his truck as he drives through the city. At each stop, his response is the same. First, he embraces as many children as he can hold and asks them how they are and what they need, digging into his pocket to give them money for food, clothing, or school supplies. "But love is what they need most," he says. "These children need love more than they need money."

Every Sunday, Fling gets up at 5:30 A.M. to go to church. The church is next door, but it takes him three hours to get there. He starts driving at 6:30 A.M., covering a fifty-five-mile circuit, collecting children as he goes.

Forty-two children later, he arrives at church, only to begin the return leg an hour later, stopping for lunch along the way. "It will be 2:30 P.M. before the kids get home, and many of them don't get breakfast," he says.

Fling doesn't have much, but he has everything. His education is limited – he only made it through the third grade – but he is wise. He has never made a lot of money, but few people with money are as rich. He has never sought public acclaim, but few people are as well respected in their communities.

"The really great men on earth are never known by their titled names, or seldom so," Harry Tippet said. So significant has been their service, so distinguished their gifts, that their simple name is enough."

When you talk to the people of Columbia, South Carolina, as I have, you know John Fling has made it. People speak his name with reverence. Newspapers call him "a good Samaritan," "a good neighbor," or "the everyday Santa." But what most people will tell you is "John Fling is a living saint."

QUESTIONS:

Who among your associates is the greatest success in economic terms? Who is the greatest success in humanistic terms? Are they the same people? If not, which one do you admire and value more?

THE MEANING OF SUCCESS

"Success is not counted by how high you have climbed
but by how many you have brought with you."

...Will Rose

Bob Pamplin believes that a successful life means living up to our God-given potential. True to his belief, Pamplin has made of himself a Renaissance man. He is a businessman and farmer, minister, and author of ten books. He holds eight degrees and has had incredible financial success.

Pamplin made his first million in the stock market as an undergraduate in the '60s. Later, he invested wisely in timber and farmlands, and now owns, along with his father, seventeen textile mills, plus a concrete and asphalt company.

A brush with cancer inspired him to enroll in a seminary. On graduation, he established his own church — the only church I know of without a congregation. The church's principal function is to provide forty-seven Northwest service agencies with food for the poor.

Pamplin supports his ministry through his farm – Twelve Oaks – making it a most unusual charity, a self-sustaining one. All of the products distributed through the church are either produced on the farm or purchased with proceeds from farm products. He sells hazelnuts, marionberries, strawberries, raspberries, and filberts to defray the cost of running the farm. Beef and produce raised on his farm are given directly to those in need.

"Businessmen have to take the entrepreneurial spirit that

they applied to business and apply it to charity," Pamplin explains. "That's what real charity is all about."

When he was thirty-three, Pamplin was diagnosed with cancer. Two years later, he was in good health, starting a new company and wondering why he was spared. The question remained open for months.

"Why me? Why was I saved?" he wondered. "Whenever I think back on that speck of tar, it is clear that God has loved me enough to apply shock treatment to my soul. His direction for my life has come in jolts, always forcing me out of my naked dependence on self and back into humble trust in him."

Pamplin believes that God blessed him with good fortune in order to set an example. In essence, God loaned him the ability to be successful. Since this ability is on loan, Pamplin decided it was his duty to pass his good fortune on to others.

"People of wealth need to make an effort to become more aware of the problems and needs of their communities," Pamplin says. "I believe that God spared me to do good. He had a use for me."

Pamplin is committed to helping members of society who are less fortunate than others, but in a creative way that allows them to become contributing partners in the society. He wants to make an investment in the total person.

"We are all important, no matter what our circumstances. It is really not the title or the material wealth that is the worth. It is the human being. Our lives aren't just surrounded by bricks and mortar and polished wood. It is the people we come into contact with every day that give our lives character. It is the people who are the soul of our society, and for our soul to have any value whatsoever, we have to live by certain principles – traditions of family unity, service to others, caring, honor, and fair dealing. Our own success, to be real, must contribute to the success of others."

QUESTIONS:

Bob Pamplin's goal is to try and fashion himself into something close to what God wants him to be. How close are you to that kind of success? Are you living up to the best that is in you? How has your success contributed to the success of others?

WHAT IS YOUR NET WORTH?

"The dead hold in their hands only what they have given away."

...Carl Sandburg

When someone asks my net worth, I never know how to reply.

I know for most people it is the measure of all that is material – all we have gathered or produced at a given point in our life. Under this scenario, when we die we cash in our chips and the grand total is pronounced. The game is over.

Albert Schweitzer suggested a different standard. At the age of eighty-five, when he was asked to provide some words to live by, he wrote the following:

It is not enough merely to exist. It is not enough to say, I'm earning enough to live and to support my family. I do my work well. I am a good father. I am a good husband. I am a good churchgoer.

*That's all very well. But you must do something more. Seek always to do some good, somewhere. Every man has to seek in his own way to make his own self more noble and to **realize his own true worth.***

In a material society, we should not be surprised when our first instinct is to measure success in economic terms. But on reflection, we know Schweitzer is nearer the truth. The measure of life is more in what we have given than in what we have gained, more in what we have passed on than in what we have kept. There are too many people of whom it could be said that "the only benefit they conferred on society was in leaving it."

The final scorecard, when all is said and done, will only for a moment measure the value of our assets. The final judgment comes down to less tangible things – lives touched, smiles given, people helped, children cared for, joy spread, love shared, and the willingness of the heart.

In these terms, John McMeel, founder and president of Universal Press Syndicate, is one of the most successful men I know. John was not brought to our attention because of his business acumen, but rather in spite of it. In fact, he was nominated by a competitor who, by conventional wisdom, should be happier if John were a little less successful.

On receiving our request for nominations, Lawrence A. Leser, CEO of E. W. Scripps Co., responded as follows: "When I looked at your material, I found a very high standard. We don't have anyone like that around here. I wish we did. The first name to come to mind was not from our company, but a competitor. I wish that were not true, because everyone should have someone like John McMeel around."

Universally described as "one of the kindest men I have ever met," John has a gift for sharing himself with those around him. He simply listens to people, sits with people, prays with people, and at times, cries with them.

John McMeel was born in South Bend, Indiana. Notre Dame, where his father was the sports teams' physician, was home. Over a kitchen table more than twenty-five years ago, he and his partner, Jim Andrews, founded the Universal Press Syndicate – now one of the largest newspaper syndication companies in the country.

"I've been very fortunate," John says. "I was born into a very special family. I've never had any real problems. I have had wonderful people in my life. Given all that, you have a feeling that you've got to give something back. You *need* to give something back. You *want* to give something back."

A few of the more visible ways John McMeel gives back are Christmas in October, which he founded to help renovate housing for the poor and elderly, and the Andrews Scholars, which he and his friends created at Notre Dame to teach kids the value of service. But his major contribution is with the quality of his life.

"No man," Henry Ward Beecher wrote, "can tell whether he is rich or poor by turning to his ledger. It is the heart that makes a man rich. He is rich according to what he is, not according to what he has." What you have on the day of your death will belong to someone else. But what you are, you will be forever.

Larry Leser was right. Everyone should have a man like John McMeel around. He demonstrates that the measure of our true worth can be found in the benefit others gain from our success.

QUESTIONS:

If one measure of success is the number you have brought with you, where do you stand? Are you alone where you are or supported by a multitude?

THE BOTTOM LINE

"No enterprise can exist for itself alone. It ministers to some great need, or performs some great service, not for itself, but for others."

...Calvin Coolidge

Fifteen years ago when we began searching for America's true heroes, we were told we would not find many businesspeople among them. From Wall Street to *Wheel of Fortune*, the media of that moment was consumed with the world of appetites. Pundits proclaimed, "The one who dies with the most toys wins," and redefined the Golden Rule to – "The one with the gold rules." We were in the midst of what has been called "the decade of greed," and everyone knew what mattered most was the bottom line.

Bottom-line managers, buttressed by the "take-no-prisoners" analysts, corporate raiders, and economic gurus promoted the perception that compassion and the free enterprise system were incompatible. The implication was that in order to succeed in business one must be completely selfish and have the instincts of an assassin.

Contrary to these dim expectations, we found there is a remarkable consistency of character that runs through the best of those in the business world. For example, when I interviewed Truett Cathy, the founder of Chick-fil-A, he was quick to point out that he insisted his business be run in a manner that was compatible with his personal philosophy. When I asked him about his accomplishments, he did not refer to the number of Chick-fil-A franchises, gross revenues, or his possessions. Instead, he quoted Scripture, telling me a good name is to be preferred to gold and silver.

Henri Landwirth arrived in this country with less than twenty dollars to his name. While he brought with him nothing material, he will tell you he had everything that matters. From Henri's heart and head, his belief in himself and the American dream, has come a fortune and the opportunity to create a miracle called Give Kids the World.

Twelve years ago, Henri made an immediate and modest response to the wish of one child with the gift of one of his hotel rooms. Now his program involves more than a hundred corporations that donate more than $14 million annually and a fifty-one-acre resort built specially for these kids. At the heart of this resort is Kids' Village, valued at more than $35 million and built without a single contract. Among other things, Henri's corporate partners demonstrate you don't have to chose between *making* and *having* a life worth living.

Every career that matters, every profession that fulfills, every business that succeeds over the long term somehow makes things better for others. There is pride and dignity in any activity that helps. There is satisfaction, joy, and fulfillment in any job worth doing.

So long as what we do contributes to the well-being of others, as Mother Teresa says, it doesn't matter *what* you do. "What matters is the love you put into what you do."

When I asked bank chairman Hugh Jones why he made the community the bank's business, Hugh said simply, "I think we all have a moral obligation to put something back." He explained that this commitment pays personal and economic dividends that the shortsighted cynics of the world cannot begin to understand.

Norb Berg, deputy chairman of the board of Control Data, put it this way. "You don't live to breathe," he said. "You breathe to live. Companies don't live to make a profit, they make a profit so they can serve people."

Bob Macauley established The Virginia Fibre Company in an attempt to set a new standard of corporate responsibility. He established a Partnership in Caring that made every employee a stakeholder. As part of this commitment, every employee shares equally in the company's profits and the entire corporation shares its profits with the world. Each year, Virginia Fibre gives away 10 percent of pre-tax profits, much of it going to support the relief efforts of AmeriCares.

From the beginning, Macauley says, he wanted his company not only to be a part of its community but also to understand its responsibility to the world. It is the leveraging of Virginia Fibre's support that has made it possible for Macauley to provide more than $2 *billion* worth of aid to those in need around the world.

Far from being the exception, Macauley, Jones, Landwirth, and Cathy represent one of the strongest currents running through our research — a solid core of American businesspeople who work to benefit others. More have been nominated for their selflessness and service than any other segment of society. These leaders demonstrate a belief best expressed by Bob Macauley that, "It is in loving and giving that we find purpose for our lives."

Macauley knows a person cannot do right in one department of life while doing wrong in another. Life is one indivisible whole. To survive, people and corporations must serve.

Americans did not invent caring, but we have certainly integrated it into our society to a degree unprecedented in the history of civilization. The concept of caring is fundamental to our system of government, inherent in our belief in the value of the individual and in the inalienable rights of man. Caring provides the justification for capitalism and the free enterprise system. It is, in fact, a distillation of the genius at the heart of America.

It reflects the enlightened self-interest that has made us strong and can sustain us as surely as greed and self-absorption can destroy us. In the words of Trammel Crow, one of our most successful developers, "A major component of every successful business is love."

That's the bottom line.

QUESTIONS

WHAT IS YOUR NET WORTH?

WOULD YOU PREFER TO BE MEASURED BY
WHAT YOU HAVE GAINED OR WHAT YOU HAVE GIVEN?

HOW WILL PEOPLE SAY SOCIETY HAS BENEFITED FROM
YOUR PRESENCE AND PARTICIPATION IN THE WORLD?

HAVE YOU MADE YOUR MARK?

HOW MANY LIVES HAVE YOU SAVED?

HOW MANY SOULS HAVE YOU NURTURED?

HOW MANY WOUNDS HAVE YOU HEALED?

HOW MANY HUNGRY HAVE YOU FED?

HOW MANY HOMELESS HAVE YOU SHELTERED?

HOW MANY CHILDREN HAVE YOU CHERISHED?

HOW MANY SMILES HAVE YOU EXCHANGED?

HOW MUCH JOY HAVE YOU ADDED?

HOW MANY PEOPLE HAVE YOU LOVED?

HAVE YOU POURED YOURSELF OUT TO OTHERS OR
KEPT YOUR LIFE TO YOURSELF?

WHAT YOU HAVE WILL BE LOST ON THE DAY OF YOUR DEATH.

WHAT YOU ARE, YOU WILL BE FOREVER.
WHAT ARE YOU AND WHAT WOULD YOU LIKE TO BE?

V

ABOUT THE TEACHERS

KENT AMOS — It Takes a Lot of Homes to Make a Village

Kent Amos, a retired consultant, has opened his home to more than eighty-seven young adults in the District of Columbia and provided them with a positive environment and a role model. Seventy-three of these teenagers have been guided from high school through college by Amos, and another eighteen are now attending college with his support.

WALLY AMOS — The Gift of Your Misfortune

Wally Amos is the founder of Uncle Noname Cookie Company. He is also the national spokesman for Literacy Volunteers of America and serves on the board of directors for Cities in Schools, Inc., a national nonprofit organization dedicated to preventing high school students from dropping out.

NORBERT BERG — The Bottom Line

As deputy chairman of the board of Control Data Corporation, Berg had the reputation of being the most innovative human resource manager in the country. Many of the programs he created for Control Data, such as

EAR (a crisis intervention service), Flextime, and Homework, have been widely copied. The community service programs he developed, including Insight (a self-supporting educational program for prison inmates), Twelve Baskets (a food distribution program), and a taxi service for runaways and lost children, have been equally well received and are still being replicated across the country.

RICHARD BLOCH — What Matters?

After successfully fighting a bout with cancer in 1978, Bloch, co-founder of H&R Block, decided to devote his life to helping others win the same battle.

RICHARD BLOCH

He started the Cancer Hot Line in Kansas City; established the R.A. Bloch Cancer Support Center at the University of Missouri, where over one hundred physicians provide second opinions to cancer victims free of charge; and created PDQ, a computer program that enables physicians to identify treatments for every form of cancer. PDQ was adopted for use by the National Cancer Institute in 1984.

M E L   B L O U N T — The Purpose of Celebrity

Blount, a former Pittsburgh Steeler, is the founder of two homes for boys aged seven through thirteen – the Mel Blount Youth Homes in Vidalia, Georgia, and Claysville, Pennsylvania. Boys who have committed petty thefts or are truants are placed in Blount's homes by social services for an average of six to eighteen months to receive counseling, schooling, discipline, and love.

J O E   C A R R O L L — Giving in to God

Bronx-born Joe Carroll has directed the formation of St. Vincent de Paul Village, one of the country's most widely replicated programs for the homeless. Just over a decade ago, Carroll conceived of and created this $11.7 million, 110,000-square-foot, state-of-the-art complex in San Diego. The Village serves more than 2,000 people a day, and provides residential services for 855 people, a medical clinic, a full range of support services designed to give a step up to the estimated 40 percent of homeless people who are "situationally homeless," and over 1 million meals a year.

PHOTO BY: ANGIE HALAMANDARIS

JOE CARROLL

JIMMY AND ROSALYNN CARTER — Our Best Ex-President

While others have retired after reaching the pinnacle of leadership to play and rest, President and Mrs. Carter have sought new ways to serve society. In 1982, Jimmy Carter founded The Carter Center at Emory University and, in 1987, Rosalynn Carter established the Rosalynn Carter Institute (RCI) for Human Development at Georgia Southwestern College. The Carter Center, which promotes world peace and international health policies, includes the Jimmy Carter Library and Museum, Global 2000 Inc., The Task Force for Child Survival and Development, the Carter-Menil Human Rights Foundation, and the Atlanta Project. RCI has extensive programs that assist caregivers of people with mental and emotional problems and those with physical illnesses associated with aging.

TRUETT CATHY

S. TRUETT CATHY — The Purpose of Life

Cathy is the founder of the Chick-fil-A company. Since 1973, Chick-fil-A has provided its employees with college scholarships totaling more than $8 million. In addition, in 1984, Cathy created the WinShape Center, which helps fund youth support programs and the WinShape Foster Care program, which provides a loving family environment for over forty-five children.

JO ANN CAYCE — The Joy of Service

Cayce has volunteered tirelessly for over forty-five years to relieve the suffering of the poor in south Arkansas. Cayce works up to twenty hours a day helping those facing difficult challenges. She is the guardian angel and advocate for the elderly, mentally and physically disabled, abused, homeless, and needy in her community.

MARY JO COPELAND — God's Hand

Copeland is the founder and director of Sharing & Caring Hands, a Minneapolis-based organization that has served the city's poor and homeless since 1985. Sharing & Caring Hands serves over five hundred people daily by providing free meals, shelter and transportation assistance, hygiene facilities, individual counseling, legal aid, and medical services.

STAN CURTIS — Everyone Has a Purpose

Curtis is the founder of Kentucky Harvest and Harvest USA. Harvest USA is the largest all-volunteer organization in the country dedicated to feeding the hungry. Curtis neither asks for nor accepts financial assistance. Instead he forges partnerships with shipping companies, hotels, airlines, and other corporations, and with a volunteer army that's fifty-seven thousand people strong. He asks for their time, their services, and their commitment, and, in so doing, has discovered a rich, untapped resource. Each day 875,000 pounds of food are distributed to 5,300 agencies, with a total of 1.5 million meals served each day.

JACQUES D'AMBOISE — The Service of Art

Jacques d'Amboise turned down an opportunity to run the New York City Ballet and the promise of a lucrative Broadway and film career to establish the National Dance Institute (NDI) in 1976. Since its inception, NDI, one of the country's largest arts education organizations, has raised self-esteem and awareness of the arts in over a half million inner-city students between the ages of nine and fifteen.

PHOTO BY: DOUG DEMARK

JESSICA DAVEY

JESSICA DAVEY—
MOTHER TERESA'S ORANGE

While in high school in Norfolk, Virginia, Davey tutored sign language, volunteered at the King's Daughter Children's Hospital, and gave more than 300 volunteer hours to Operation Smile's youth organization, the Happy Club. In her sophomore year of college, Jessica fulfilled a lifelong ambition to meet and work with Mother Teresa. She has since returned to India eight times, and now at age twenty-six, she is attending the London School of Economics.

EVELYN duPONT * — WALKING ON WATER

Evelyn duPont began teaching handicapped people to swim in the early 1950s. She began in her backyard pool and then founded California Pools for the Handicapped (CPH) in 1963. Her program, which offers free pool services and rehabilitation to anyone with a disability, has benefited more than 350,000 individuals.

YVONNE FEDDERSON AND SARA O'MEARA—
GOD WILL GET YOU

Fedderson and O'Meara founded International Orphans, Inc., in 1961 to help orphaned Amerasian children in Japan and Vietnam. In 1978 their focus shifted to the plight of abused children in the United States and they founded Children's Village USA, the first residential treatment center established for the victims of child abuse and neglect.

ARTHUR FLEMMING * — A HAPPY DEATH

The consummate public servant, Flemming received his first presidential appointment from Franklin Delano Roosevelt in 1939. He served seven presidents in all, chaired numerous federal commissions, was a member of the two Hoover Commissions, and was appointed secretary of Health, Education and Welfare by President Eisenhower.

JOHN FLING — THE SAINT OF SOUTH CAROLINA

Fling has devoted twelve- to fifteen-hour days, every day, for the past forty years to serving those in need. He cares for an extended family that includes some four hundred underprivileged children, two hundred seniors, and forty blind people, and responds to dozens of calls every day from people who need his help.

VIKTOR FRANKL — A SIGN FROM GOD

Viktor Frankl, M.D., Ph.D., is the author of *Man's Search for Meaning*, an international bestseller, and thirty other books. His works have been translated into twenty-four languages.

VIKTOR FRANKL

MILLARD FULLER — EVERYONE CAN BE GREAT

Fuller is the founder of Habitat for Humanity. Since 1976, Habitat for Humanity, a nonprofit organization made up of volunteers who assist the underprivileged in building their own homes, has organized over 378 affiliated projects in the United States, Canada, and South Africa and more than seventy-one projects in twenty-six

MILLARD FULLER

developing countries. Habitat has grown to become the one of the largest home builders in the United States and the sixth largest builder of homes in the world.

B E A   G A D D Y — The Sky's the Limit

Gaddy founded the Patterson Park Emergency Food Center, which she operates from her home, providing food for nearly four hundred people every day. She has created over a dozen programs to help the poor in Baltimore, including the Bea Gaddy Women and Children's Center, a transitional housing program for homeless women and children. She also hosts and organizes annually the largest Thanksgiving dinner in America, feeding more than twenty thousand people each year.

J O H N   G A R D N E R — The Kindness of Strangers

Former secretary of the Department of Health, Education and Welfare, Gardner has served as advisor to six presidents. Gardner founded two national civic groups, Common Cause and the Independent Sector, and is the author of seven books including three best-sellers: *Self Renewal*, *Leadership*, and *Excellence*.

PHOTO BY: C. BOEHM

JANE GOODALL

J A N E   G O O D A L L — The Gift of the Forest

Best known for her pioneering research work with chimpanzees, Jane Goodall is also a strong believer that, together, we can effect global change. This belief forms the basis of the Jane Goodall Institute (JGI), which she founded in 1977. One of JGI's seventeen programs is Roots and Shoots, which involves over fifteen thousand students worldwide. JGI's other programs provide for ongoing wildlife research, education, and conservation projects, such as a Tanzanian reforestation program and the Gombe Stream Research Center.

"Sweet" Alice Harris — You Can't Beat God at Giving

Harris has worked to improve conditions for minorities in the Watts area of Los Angeles for more than thirty-five years. She is the founder of Parents of Watts, which offers fifteen programs to the community, including a program for young mothers, legal counseling for parents and children, emergency food and shelter assistance for the homeless, and educational classes.

Corla Hawkins — The Greatest Sin

For two decades Corla Hawkins has been teaching children in one of Chicago's worst neighborhoods. But to her children, Momma Hawk is much more than a teacher. She is mother and mentor, savior and self-esteem raiser. She begins each day by cooking them breakfast and ends the school day by taking most of them home with her. She spends 40 percent of her own take-home salary in the care and feeding of these children.

Harriet Hodges — The Key to Happiness

Hodges, director of the International Human Assistance Program, is an American citizen and wife of a career Army officer who has spent much of her life stationed abroad. For the past twenty years she has helped secure necessary heart surgery in the United States for thousands of Korean children who cannot obtain the care they need in their own country.

Jon Huntsman — The Greatest Gift

In 1995 Jon Huntsman provided a $100 million endowment to find a cure for cancer. While the size of this bequest was significant, it was by no means out of character for the president of the Huntsman Corporation. Over the years, Huntsman has quietly but significantly supported causes as varied as the Jake Garn Institute, Utah State's environmental research center, the Bennion Center, Armenian earthquake victims, and Catholic Charities, among others.

GERALD JAMPOLSKY, M.D., AND DIANE CIRINCIONE — THE GIFT OF YOUR MISFORTUNE

Jampolsky and Cirincione are the driving force behind the fifty worldwide Centers for Attitudinal Healing, which have been in existence since 1975. The centers support children with disabilities and life-threatening illnesses as well as adults facing catastrophic conditions. They are also the founders of Children as Teachers of Peace, an organization that provides a mechanism for children to express their feelings, ideas, hopes, and desires for a better world.

KEVIN JOHNSON — THE ESSENCE OF LIFE

Johnson, a basketball player with the Phoenix Suns, founded St. Hope Academy in Sacramento in 1989 for underprivileged children. Twenty children take part in the day academy, which provides for the child's basic needs as well as academics and character building. In Phoenix, Johnson has

instituted KJ's Readers and serves on the board of directors of the Phoenix Suns Charities and the School House Foundation.

HUGH JONES — LOVE IS THE BRIDGE

As chairman and chief executive officer of Barnett Bank in Jacksonville, Florida, Hugh Jones established a corporate philosophy that encouraged bank employees to be responsible citizens. In response, employees contributed over forty thousand hours a year to community projects. Jones set

HUGH JONES

the example by his involvement in many social service programs, including the Korean Heart Program, INROADS, Ronald McDonald House, and the United Way of Jacksonville. He is currently president of the Baptist Health Systems Foundation and one of the principle forces behind the creation of a homeless shelter for Jacksonville.

DR. LARRY JONES — I'd Rather Be a Sermon

In 1979, Larry Jones founded Feed the Children, an international nonprofit hunger and disaster relief organization operating in sixty-seven countries. Feed the Children provides over eighty thousand people with daily supplemental meals and provides clothing, medical care, and supplies to persons suffering as a result of poverty or natural disaster.

RICHARD JULIAN — Hear the Whisper

Now twenty-three years old, Julian was the driving force behind many community service activities throughout high school and college. During his senior year of high school in Greenville, South Carolina, Rick, who was then homeless, spent more than 400 hours volunteering with many programs, including the American Cancer Society, Drug Awareness Resistance Education, Special Olympics, and Project Host Soup Kitchen. Over the last decade, Rick has also helped coordinate activities that raised over $20,000 for Children's Hospital and $25,000 for Camp Spearhead for handicapped children.

SISTER MARY LUCA JUNK * — The Golden Years

For more than twenty years, Sister Mary Luca was the angel of mercy for the poor of the barrio. She organized a back-to-school clothing drive that provided two sets of school attire each year for each of ten thousand children. She established English classes, arranged funerals, obtained legal aid, and provided emergency food and funds for rent and medicine.

M A R Y A N N E   K E L L Y — WHEN THE SOUL COMES ALIVE

Kelly founded the Centre for Living with Dying in 1976 to provide community resources to assist people in dealing with isolation of loss, grief, and death. Over 180,000 people have received support through the Centre's community outreach and education programs.

PHOTO BY: ANGIE HALAMANDARIS

RANYA KELLY

R A N Y A   K E L L Y — LEARN TO LOVE

Over the last ten years, Ranya, a Denver housewife and mother, has distributed more than 150,000 pairs of shoes to those in need. She is the founder of The Redistribution Center, which, while operating out of her home on an annual budget of twelve thousand dollars, distributes over $2 million worth of clothing, food, building and medical supplies, linens, and toys to needy organizations in Colorado and neighboring states.

HENRI LANDWIRTH

H E N R I   L A N D W I R T H — THE DESIGN OF THE UNIVERSE

Co-owner of a string of Holiday Inns in central Florida, Landwirth arrived in this country in 1950 with twenty dollars in his pocket. A survivor of the Holocaust, he has dedicated himself to others, creating the Fanny Landwirth Foundation for seniors, helping establish the *Mercury 7* Foundation for promising students, and organizing Give Kids the World, an organization that fulfills the last wish of over four thousand terminally ill children and their families each year.

E U G E N E   M .   L A N G — A Beautiful Dream

Lang created the "I Have a Dream" program in 1981 when he addressed a group of graduating sixth graders in east Harlem. Four years later, Lang established the national I Have a Dream Foundation (IHAD), a partnership of individuals and organizations committed to motivating disadvantaged students to stay in school. IHAD has helped more than twelve thousand dreamers around the country finance their college education through individually sponsored projects in more than fifty-three cities in twenty-seven states.

L O I S   L E E — Unconditional Love

Lee's research on her doctoral dissertation in 1975 taught her that many prostitutes were teens running away from incest and abuse. Her research inspired her to establish a program called Children of the Night to help kids escape prostitution and pornography. Children of the Night now operates a shelter, a walk-in crisis center, a street outreach program, counseling, crisis intervention, a job placement service, and several group homes. To date, COTN has rescued over eight thousand children from the streets.

E D I T H   L E W I S * — There Are No Bad Kids

Lewis, founder of Grandma's House, spent the last twenty years of her life giving love and a second chance to abused and traumatized youth. She provided a home to hundreds of troubled youths, ages eighteen to twenty-three, labeled "lost causes" by society. Eighty percent of the young men and women were successfully turned around.

PHOTO BY: ANGIE HALAMANDARIS

GRANDMA EDIE

ROBERT MACAULEY

ROBERT MACAULEY —
THE URGENCY OF NOW

Chairman of The Virginia Fibre Company, Macauley established the Shoeshine Foundation in 1968, which provided shelter and long-term care for more than twenty-five hundred orphaned Vietnamese children, and served as chairman of the board of Covenant House. He is also the chairman and founder of AmeriCares, which since 1982 has provided $2 billion worth of medicine and supplies to desperately needy people around the world.

PHOTO BY: ANGIE HALAMANDARIS

BILL & KATHY MAGEE

BILL & KATHY MAGEE
— THE GIFT OF WHAT YOU DO

For fourteen years, Bill and Kathy Magee have been bringing smiles to faces around the globe. Bill, a craniofacial specialist, and Kathy, a nurse and social worker, founded Operation Smile in 1982. Since then Operation Smile has organized over 120 medical missions to fifteen countries and performed over eighteen thousand surgeries abroad and another twenty-one thousand surgeries here in the United States.

FERDINAND MAHFOOD — THE KEY TO HAPPINESS

Mahfood is the founder and president of Food for the Poor, which works to improve the health, economic, spiritual, and social conditions of the underprivileged in developing countries and in the United States. Since 1982

Food for the Poor has provided over $110 million worth of aid and has established numerous programs providing job training aimed at developing self-sufficiency.

FRED MATSER — The Dance

Matser has established and supports programs around the world through his People for People Foundation for Environmental Awareness. He lends support to numerous activities worldwide, including a clinic for AIDS babies in Romania, medical and social programs and agricultural projects for the people in Surinam, the Martagao Gesteira Children's Hospital in Brazil (where more than one thousand kids are seen daily), a home for Tibetan orphans, and the Primary Health Care Center in Tanzania.

JACK MCCONNELL — Caring Is Contagious

McConnell was one of the driving forces behind the development of medical inventions as remarkable as the TB Tyne test, Tylenol, and the MRI. In his retirement, McConnell conceived of a clinic staffed by retired physicians, nurses, dentists, and lay people that would provide high-quality free medical care to those in need on Hilton Head Island, South Carolina. Since it opened its doors 1994, Volunteers in Medicine has treated seven thousand patients.

MONSIGNOR IGNATIUS MCDERMOTT — Compassion

Father McDermott has been helping the homeless of Chicago, particularly those with alcohol and drug abuse problems, for over fifty years. After years of helping his friends on skid row, McDermott founded Haymarket House, the first free-standing, social-setting detoxification center in Illinois. Haymarket House has since expanded to a large complex known as the McDermott Center, which houses 325 men and 175 women in private rooms. "Mac Hilton" includes a detoxification center, food and shelter for the homeless, counseling, drug abuse services, family involvement, and a maternal addiction unit.

L E E A N N E M c G R A T H — A World of Possibilities

PHOTO BY: ANGIE HALAMANDARIS

LEEANNE MCGRATH

Leeanne McGrath's Sharing Connection provides a vital link between caring people and people who need care. Its establishment in 1987 transformed McGrath's suburban home into an overflowing redistribution center for clothing, furniture, baby items and toys, and food. Some three dozen Chicago service organizations now come to McGrath for assistance. She has also found a way to aid children in Romania, Mexico, Haiti, Bosnia, and Honduras.

J O H N M c M E E L — What Is Your Net Worth?

Cofounder of the Universal Press Syndicate, McMeel helped establish the Andrews Scholars program at the University of Notre Dame over fifteen years ago. This program encourages students to become more involved in community social service projects across the country. In addition, in 1984 McMeel and a friend founded Christmas in October in Kansas City, which has repaired more than two thousand homes in the community.

B I L L M I L L I K E N — Love's Way

Milliken initiated the first street academies for young people who were failed by traditional schooling. Milliken saw the success of nontraditional education and started various programs in the 1970s that provided aid to young people in need. These organizations served as important predecessors to Cities in

Schools (CIS), the nation's largest nonprofit dropout prevention program, cofounded by Milliken in 1976.

N A N C Y   M I N T I E — The Happiest Lawyer in the World

Upon graduating from law school, Mintie founded the Inner City Law Center in Los Angeles. From that first day in 1980 when the city's homeless and poor lined up outside her storefront practice in space bartered from a local soup kitchen, Mintie has been their stalwart defender. The Center serves more than thirty-six hundred clients a year, with judgments and settlements for each client averaging more than one hundred thousand dollars.

M O T H E R   T E R E S A * — Radiate God's Love

Mother Teresa became known to the world for her selfless work with the "poorest of the poor" in Calcutta. Since its inception in 1950, her order, the Missionaries of Charity, has opened 500 centers around the world to help the dying and destitute.

PHOTO BY: MARILU PITTMAN-SHERER

MOTHER TERESA

H E N R Y   N I C O L S — A Profile in Courage

Nicols, a hemophiliac, tested HIV-positive almost a decade ago. In 1990, Nicols developed full-blown AIDS. He publicly disclosed his illness in Cooperstown, New York, a city of only 2,700. Nicols, who risked public humiliation and ostracism, received overwhelming support from his community and has gone on to present an AIDS education program to tens of thousands of students in schools across the state and the nation. He is now twenty-five years old.

ROBERT PAMPLIN

DR. ROBERT B. PAMPLIN, JR.—
THE MEANING OF SUCCESS

Successful businessman and founder of the Christ Community Church in Lake Oswego, Pamplin has helped thousands of people through his company and his church. One of the ministries of the church is to provide thirty-seven relief agencies with food, including beef, bread, peanut butter, eggs, fruits, and vegetables. The R. B. Pamplin Corporation donates 10 percent of its pretax profits to charity.

NORMAN VINCENT PEALE* — THE POWER OF ONE

Dr. Peale authored thirty-nine books, including the bestseller *The Power of Positive Thinking*. He was also the coeditor and publisher with his wife of *Guideposts*, the inspirational magazine, and pastor of Marble Collegiate Church in New York.

MITZI PERDUE

MITZI PERDUE—
LIFESTYLES OF THE RICH AND FAMOUS

Perdue is a leading businesswoman and syndicated columnist who has dedicated her life to a wide variety of community service activities. She is the founder and national chair of Youth Engaged in Service!, a community service youth program currently operating in over one hundred schools. She raises funds and volunteers for a number of charities, including a rehabilitation center, the Red Cross, and the Salisbury, Maryland, Zoo's "Fun(d) for Kids."

MELISSA POE — THE CHOICE

Melissa Poe began her campaign for a cleaner environment at the age of eight. She founded Kids for a Cleaner Environment (Kids FACE) in 1989 and was one of six children invited to speak at the Earth Summit in Brazil in 1992.

RACHEL WHEELER ROSSOW — EVERYONE MAKES A DIFFERENCE

Rossow provides a loving home to twenty-one exceptional children. Eighteen of these children were born with severe mental and physical handicaps and have thrived under Rossow's care. In addition, Rossow serves as a consultant with the State of Connecticut Department of Children and Youth Services, finding foster parents for children who have tested HIV-positive.

VANTREASE RUSSELL — THE GIFT OF A CHILD

Vantrease Russell has been "mother" to over twelve hundred children who have lived with her at The Russell Home for Children. At any given time, Russell's house is home to at least twenty-seven "children," some of whom have been with her for forty-five years.

MELISSA POE

VANTREASE RUSSELL

RITA UNGARO SCHIAVONE — THE GIFT OF WHO YOU ARE

Founder and administrator of Aid for Friends, Schiavone has been in community service for more than a quarter of a century. Since she founded Aid

RITA UNGARO SCHIAVONE

for Friends in 1974 to give food and friendship to the homebound, the organization has grown to a network of thousands. Aid for Friends' volunteer cooks provide over eight hundred thousand meals to people in need each year.

M I M I   S I L B E R T — Serving Time

PHOTO BY: ANGIE HALAMANDARIS

MIMI SILBERT

Twenty-five years ago, Mimi Silbert founded the Delancey Street Foundation, an organization dedicated to helping change the lives of society's castaways. Over eleven thousand criminal offenders and homeless people have since successfully completed the four-year program at five sites nationwide. Every resident must earn a GED, serve as a role model for other residents, volunteer, and learn three marketable skills. Those skills have been parlayed by the residents into a group of businesses that earns $6 million annually to support the foundation.

B E C K Y   A N D   B O B B Y   S I M P S O N — Little Miracles

Following severe flooding in 1977, the Simpsons founded the Cranks Creek Survival Center in Kentucky. Becky, who has a third-grade education, runs the Survival Center. Bobby, who is blind, coordinates the pick-up of donations and oversees all building and repair projects. The center now provides food, clothing, shelter, and educational assistance to hundreds of people in the area.

DAVID SOUKUP — The First Rule of Caring

Soukup established the first Court Appointed Special Advocate (CASA) program in 1972. CASA volunteers are trained private citizens who monitor legal cases involving abused or neglected children. They follow what is happening in the children's lives, and represent the children in court. Today twenty-eight thousand volunteers are serving approximately ninety-one thousand children annually.

JOHN STEINBRUCK — Separateness

The N Street Village was founded twenty-three years ago when John Steinbruck, pastor of Luther Place, opened the doors of his church to the homeless. Today, N Street Village provides around-the-clock refuge for Washington, D.C.'s homeless. A myriad of programs provide temporary and permanent shelter, food and medical care, assistance in addiction recovery, and training in life skills to over one thousand women each year.

DAVE THOMAS — It Starts with 'We'

Thomas, founder of Wendy's International, is the nation's leading advocate for adoption. He served as national spokesperson for the Presidential Initiative on Adoption in 1991 and is the founder of the Dave Thomas Foundation for Adoption. Thomas, who was adopted himself, has starred in PSAs promoting adoption. Proceeds from the sale of his books go to the campaign. Thomas launched a benefits program at Wendy's that gives adoptive parents the same benefits as birth parents. He encourages other companies to do the same.

DAVE THOMAS

J O H N   V A N   H E N G E L — Caring and Sharing

Van Hengel is the founder of St. Mary's—the world's first food bank. In 1976 Van Hengel founded Second Harvest, which counsels people who are interested in setting up food banks and taps into disposal programs at the manufacturing level.

D O N N A L E E   V E L V I C K — Stepping Out on Faith

Velvick established Hope House in 1973 for abused, neglected, and abandoned children. Hope House consists of four homes on nearly seventy-five acres of land near Boise, Idaho. Currently, sixty-nine children live in Hope House – many of whom are severely handicapped or struggling with mental and emotional problems. Velvick has adopted nineteen of the children and serves as legal guardian to another twenty.

K U R T   W E I S H A U P T — The Gift of Life

Weishaupt and his wife fled Nazi Germany and made their way to New York in 1941. As soon as he had established himself, he began giving back—fulfilling a promise that he had made to himself to repay the kindness of the many strangers who had helped save his life. Among the dozens of charities he supports are the Salvation Army, the March of Dimes, the YMCA, the United Jewish Appeal, and the Gift of Life, which he has chaired for sixteen years.

H A T T I E   W I L L I A M S * — Divine Thunderbolts

Williams gave everything she had to her community. Her house was a home for all those who needed a place to talk or study, as well as a clearinghouse for food, clothes, and furniture. She organized tutoring programs for elementary school children and high school dropouts, developed community gardens, and stocked a library in her basement with donated books.

TOMMIE LEE WILLIAMS — The Eye of the Heart

Williams has been serving the needs of his community for over twenty-four years through the distribution of food, clothing, job counseling, and educational services at We Care Community Services, Inc. This nonprofit organization serves the needs of over three thousand people annually in Warren County, Mississippi.

* deceased

ACKNOWLEDGMENTS

Literally hundreds of people contributed in some measure to the preparation of this book. While I cannot acknowledge them all, I would like to thank my brother, Val Halamandaris, and Senator Frank E. Moss not only for their contributions to the process that led to this book but also for their contributions to who I am. Colleen Noland coordinated the research and review effort while Marian Sprague supervised the screening and selection of candidates for interview. In both cases, this was a commitment of many hours over many years. I am deeply indebted to them both. In addition, I am grateful to Jim Agee, Ev Barnes, Kathleen Brown, Alana Calfee, Kara Everly, Ann Hill, Victoria Padgett, and Laura Sheehan for their help in researching candidates; and Hugh H. Jones, Jr., Mary Pellettieri, Colleen Noland, and Marian Sprague for their editorial assistance, insights, and encouragement. Finally, I would like to acknowledge my agent, Bob Silverstein; my editor at Longstreet Press, Sherry Wade; and my wife, Angela. Thank you for believing in this project, Sherry and Bob, and for helping to make it better. Thank you, Angie, for believing in me and helping to make me better. You are the light of my life.